TOOLS of
the Old and New
Stone Age

The Natural History Press, publisher for The American Museum of Natural History, is a division of Doubleday and Company, Inc. Directed by a joint editorial board made up of members of the staff of both the Museum and Doubleday, the Natural History Press publishes books and periodicals in all branches of the life and earth sciences, including anthropology and astronomy. The Natural History Press has its editorial offices at The American Museum of Natural History, Central Park West at Seventy-ninth Street, New York, New York 10024, and its business offices at 501 Franklin Avenue, Garden City, New York 11531.

This contemporary Turkish knapper is flaking flint blades similar to those made during the Upper Paleolithic. Today, they are used to line the bottoms of threshing sledges drawn by animals over the harvested wheat to separate the grain and chop up the stalks.

TOOLS of the Old and New Stone Age

JACQUES BORDAZ

Photographs by Lee Boltin

PUBLISHED FOR

The American Museum of Natural History

THE NATURAL HISTORY PRESS

GARDEN CITY, NEW YORK

Portions of this book are based on two articles written by the author which appeared in *Natural History* magazine in January and February, 1959. Permission to use this material is hereby gratefully acknowledged.

The final line illustrations for this book, except where otherwise noted, were prepared by the Graphic Arts Division of The American Museum of Natural History.

TOOLS OF THE OLD AND NEW STONE AGE was published simultaneously in hardbound and paperback editions by the Natural History Press.

9   8   7   6   5   4   3   2

JACQUES BORDAZ received his B.A. from the University of Paris in 1944 and his Ph.D. in anthropology from Columbia University in 1964. He has done field work in the United States, Mexico, Iraq and, more recently, in Turkey where, in 1964 and 1965, he directed the excavation of the Neolithic village site of Suberde. His current field work is located in the Lake Beyşehir region of Turkey and is sponsored by the University of Montreal and the Canada Council. He is presently Associate Professor of Anthropology at the University of Montreal.

LEE BOLTIN has served as photographer for The American Museum of Natural History, The Metropolitan Museum of Art, and The Smithsonian Institution. His photographs have appeared in a variety of magazines and journals, among them *Life, Natural History, Horizon,* and *Art Library.* Two of the more recent books he has illustrated are TREASURES OF ANCIENT AMERICA and THE MINERAL KINGDOM.

Contents

Preface

When the editors of Natural History Press offered to republish my two articles on prehistoric stone tools written ten years ago for *Natural History* magazine, I was pleased to have the opportunity to include recent discoveries, amplify the original text in many parts, add new illustrations, and generally to tell in a fuller and more detailed fashion than was possible in the magazine the interesting story of the development of man's first tools.

The book will attempt to give in a simple and concise way a résumé of our knowledge concerning the manufacture and use of prehistoric stone implements in the Old World which started about two million years ago.

Much is still unknown or problematic about stone implements particularly with respect to their function. More precise data is still needed especially from excavations and from the microscopic study of the patterns of wear on the edges of stone implements.

The manufacture of stone implements is relatively better known though much essential information is still lacking particularly on the stone waste from flint knapping sites.

I have drawn largely on the experimental stone knapping and observations of prehistoric stone tools by Alfred S. Barnes, François Bordes, Léon Coutier, Donald E. Crabtree, Francis H. S. Knowles, L. S. B. Leakey and D. F. W. Baden-Powell, who have been able to duplicate many prehistoric tools and to suggest the most likely ways in which prehistoric men might have produced them.

Professor F. Bordes was kind enough to provide me with some very useful comments on the two original articles; Professor Philip E. L. Smith read a draft of this book and made many excellent suggestions. I would like to thank them both very much.

I would also like to thank warmly Mr. Lee Boltin for his skill and patience while making the photographs of the artifacts. All photographs were taken by him except for the cover, the frontispiece, and the picture of a Solutrean laurel leaf from Volgu on page 79 which was copied from the original publication by François Chabas in 1874.

I am also very grateful to Dr. Harry L. Shapiro who loaned me the stone artifacts from the collections of the American Museum of Natural History and to the George W. Gate Co. from whom I borrowed the sodium vapor lamps used for lighting the stone implements according to a method first developed by G. Tendron.

The majority of the drawings have been prepared by Mr. Marcel Smit, Department of Anthropology, University of Montreal. Many thanks are due to him as well as to Miss Enid Kotschnig who has drawn figures 48 and 50 for one of the original articles. I would also like to express my appreciation to Professor H. D. Sankalia, University of Poona, India, for the permission to draw figures 3–6.

I am particularly indebted to John Purcell who first suggested the two articles for *Natural History* magazine while he was editor and gave me encouragement and editorial assistance.

I am also grateful to Mrs. Joan Gordan and Mr. George Barré for their assistance with the preparation of the bibliography.

Finally for editorial help with the present book, I would like to thank warmly Mrs. Victoria von Hagen as well as Mrs. Elizabeth Knappman and Mrs. Kate Brown, editors at Natural History Press, and the staff of the Press for their assistance with the preparation of the typescript for publication.

TOOLS of
the Old and New
Stone Age

I

Introduction

Only two centuries ago both the origin and nature of the objects to be presented on these pages were generally misunderstood. Mankind's long use of metal had virtually obliterated the memory of stone as a material for the manufacture of tools and weapons: the axes, arrowheads, and other surviving implements of the Stone Age were then believed, instead, to be works of nature. Over most of the Old World, indeed, they were usually referred to as "thunderstones" or "thunderbolts," in the belief that they represented the end product of a lightning flash. In certain parts of Scandinavia and France, this belief was still held during the last century, and the *pierres de foudre* were hopefully placed in the walls or under the doorsills of farmhouses in an attempt to deceive lightning, which, as was well known, never struck twice in the same place. Nor was this mere peasant superstition: early scholars called these stones "ceraunias" (from the Greek *keraunos,* thunderbolt) and proposed the most complex explanations as to which proportions of humidity, solar and stellar radiation, and lightning had produced the strange objects. Since so many apparently reliable observers had stated for centuries that they had found ceraunias at the very place where lightning had struck, little attention was given to a seventeenth-century mineralogist, Boece de Boot, who suggested that, in view of the unique form of the ceraunias, they might have been iron implements which had turned into stone through the ages.

It was not until the end of the first quarter of the eighteenth century, as a late-ripening fruit of the Age of Exploration, that the "thunderstone" belief was vanquished by the scientific evidence of the true nature of these stone objects.

The naturalist Antoine de Jussieu, in a memoir entitled *De l'origine et des usages de la pierre de foudre,* pointed out that some stone objects from the West Indies and Canada, which were known to have been manufactured and used by the aborigines of these regions as tools and weapons, were very similar to the European ceraunias, and that it was probable that the early inhabitants of Europe had also manufactured tools and weapons of stone. Still, it required almost another hundred and fifty years, until the second half of the nineteenth century, before that period known to prehistorians as the "Stone Age" was recognized as representing a vast span of time in man's history. It is a period now estimated to have lasted perhaps more than four hundred times longer than the five thousand years that have passed since the spread of metallurgical techniques from the Near East.

Of all the known activities of man during these years, we most readily appreciate the many cave paintings of the Upper Paleolithic found in southwestern Europe. Their magnificence, boldness and beauty, the aesthetic emotions these works evoke in us, erase the enormities of intervening time. Prehistoric stone implements possess a beauty of another kind. Admirably adapted to their purpose, they are pleasing in their elegant solution of the relationship between form and function. The form, texture and workmanship of many of them transcend their prosaic uses.

The major concern of scholars specializing in prehistoric stone implements has been with typological studies, that is the analysis of recurrent forms, which, in conjunction with geochronological evidence, leads to chronological and regional classifications of the ancient human societies that produced these tools. In contrast, this book is concerned with the uses to which these tools may have been put and the ways in which they were produced.

Before we start our study, it will be useful to discuss briefly the various schemes used to divide the two million years during which stone tools and weapons were used.

Man evolves in the period that geologists call the Quaternary. The Quaternary, which started with a general cooling of the climate and certain changes in marine and land fauna, is estimated to have begun two to three million years ago. It is usually divided into the Pleistocene epoch, or "the great ice age," and the Holocene, or recent epoch that started with post-glacial times about 10,000 years ago. The Pleistocene has itself been further subdivided into stages according to the geological evidence for glacial and pluvial fluctuations and the concurrent faunal and floral changes.

Interpretation of this evidence is difficult and several sets of subdivisions have been proposed, none of which can be considered final at this time. The scheme to be used here was chosen because it divides the Pleistocene into the most parts, i.e. four instead of the usual three. The first, the Basal Pleistocene, began with the first sign of a colder climate, between two and three million years ago. The onset of the second part, the Lower Pleistocene is set about 500,000 years ago; it lasted for almost 200,000 years. The third part, the Middle Pleistocene, ran from 275,000 to 100,000 years ago. The fourth and last part, the Upper Pleistocene, began 100,000 years ago and ended about 10,000 years ago when the Holocene or post-glacial epoch started.

Figure 1 shows the subdivisions of the Pleistocene according to the four part scheme and their dates which, it must be stressed, are quite tentative particularly in the early phase of the Pleistocene. The glacial and interglacial stages are indicated on the chart. The names used are those which have been given to the glacial advances which took place in the European Alps. They were the first to be studied and have since been traditionally used as reference points for all subsequent studies of climatic variations during the Pleistocene epoch.

In addition to classifying the Pleistocene according to environmental evidence, archaelogists have developed a subdivision based on the archaeological evidence itself. It relies on the shape and method of manufacture of stone implements and their relative proportions within the collections from the Quaternary layers. This traditional archaeological classification, called the *Three Age system,* divides the archaeological record into three parts: the Stone Age, the Bronze Age, and the Iron Age.

The Stone Age, with which we are concerned here, has itself been subdivided into three periods: the Paleolithic ("Old stone"), the Mesolithic ("Middle stone"), and the Neolithic ("New

YEARS AGO (X 1000)	GLACIATIONS (ALPS)	GEOLOGICAL DIVISIONS	ARCHAEOLOGICAL DIVISIONS
	Postglacial	Holocene	Neolithic Mesolithic
10			
	Würm	Upper Pleistocene	Upper Paleolithic
35			
			Middle Paleolithic
75			
100			
	Riss	Middle Pleistocene	
200			
275			
	Mindel	Lower Pleistocene	
500			
	Günz		Lower Paleolithic
		Basal Pleistocene	
	Donau and Earlier Stages		
2000			

Figure 1.

stone")—a nomenclature that refers to the manner in which stone implements were made. Thus, during the Paleolithic, which lasted the length of the Pleistocene, stone implements were shaped by flaking only. The Paleolithic is usually subdivided, as shown in *Figure* 1, into three parts: lower, middle, and upper— each subdivision characterized by the major types of tool-flaking techniques.

The Mesolithic is considered to be an intermediate period, spanning immediate post-glacial times. It was followed by the Neolithic in which the technique of shaping tools by grinding was introduced.

It is evident that certain of these stone-shaping techniques overlap defined periods. Blade tools, for instance, which were dominant in the Upper Paleolithic, are also found in earlier collections. Conversely, techniques characteristic of early times trail into later ones. Thus, we find that stone flaking was still used extensively during the Neolithic.

The three main technological subdivisions correlate broadly with the major types of subsistence: the Paleolithic is restricted to hunting, fishing, and gathering cultures; the Neolithic is characterized by agriculture and herding; and the Mesolithic includes societies which in some parts of the world combined Paleolithic types of subsistence with the first beginnings of agriculture and herding.

The reader should note that the passage from one type of stone-shaping technique to a new one often takes place with considerable delay in different parts of the world. This is because it takes time for economic or technical innovations to spread from the original center of development to more distant or particularly conservative regions. Here, boundaries tend to be somewhat arbitrary and overlapping exists.

Despite its shortcomings, the traditional archaeological scheme is quite useful for presenting the long development of stone tools and weapons in broad terms. Hopefully, however, as the results of archaeological research accrue, additional criteria such as the type and relative permanence of settlements and the relative importance of the various types of subsistence, can be used to establish less arbitrary divisions of the prehistoric time scale, thus permitting a more detailed and more culturally significant picture of the development of prehistoric societies.

II
Stone Tool Materials

For nearly two million years during the glacial and early post-glacial times, man managed to survive and to populate all the inhabitable regions of the earth. Initially he was a food-gatherer who hunted, fished and collected wild plants; and later, beginning in the Middle East about 9000 years ago, he became a food producer who farmed and herded.

During all this time, stone was man's principal aid in exploiting nature, and his progress in this exploitation was associated with technological advances in stone implements. These advances followed two main trends. First, there was an evolution in the forms and an increase in the number of the implements, which were developed from a few generalized all-purpose tools and weapons to more specialized and better adapted ones. Second, there was an evolution in the mode of their manufacture. Man was learning to make better use of suitable raw material: he not only reduced waste but also developed new techniques which enabled him to utilize a greater variety of materials for the manufacture of stone weapons and tools.

Stone was not the only material used by Stone Age man. The rarity of bone, antler, and wood artifacts, especially in archaeological collections is obviously due to the fact that these materials decay rapidly. Upper Paleolithic implements of antler and bone, such as spears or harpoon points, have been collected from rock shelters and caves where conditions are usually more favorable for preservation of organic material than at open air sites. The preservation of wooden artifacts usually requires ever more unusual conditions, such as those found in the Scandinavian Mesolithic peat-bog site or the waterlogged site of Kalambo

Falls in Northern Rhodesia. It was at Kalambo Falls that rough wooden sticks (presumably digging sticks and clubs) approximately 60,000 years old were discovered.

Even earlier finds of wooden stick fragments showing human workmanship have since been found at the late Lower Pleistocene site of Torralba in Spain. Roughly contemporary with the Torralba finds, which date to about 300,000 years ago, is the point of a yew spear unearthed at Clacton-on-Sea, in England. The most spectacular early wooden artifact discovered was found at the site of Lehringen, West Germany, and dates to the early part of the Upper Pleistocene, 80,000 years ago. It is a broken but complete eight-foot yew spear, with a fire-hardened point and what appear to be finger notches.

Thus, although wood is a rarely preserved tool material, it is obvious that it must have been widely used from earliest prehistoric times.

Although bone and antler are more resistant to decay, they are harder to work and the evidence seems to indicate that prior to Upper Paleolithic times, these materials were seldom used and then only for very roughly shaped implements. Long bones and horns can serve as weapons without prior modification, and there is a good possibility that the earliest man of the Basal Pleistocene made use of them. From the Lower Pleistocene on, finds of roughly flaked or split long bones showing signs of wear are not unusual, and many more have probably escaped notice. The earliest of such artifacts (from the upper part of the Lower Pleistocene) have been found at Chou-kou-tien in China, at Olduvai Gorge in Tanzania, and at Torralba and Ambrona in Spain.

The fact that stone is practically indestructible, and hence constitutes almost the totality of the artifacts recovered, should not lead us to forget that stone was only one of the materials used by ancient man.

Stone tools were certainly the most important part of the equipment of early man. They alone provided him with the working edge and the point he needed for cutting, chopping, scraping, piercing and preparing the now largely vanished materials: wood, bone, antler, sinew, and skin, which comprised the remainder, and possibly, the major part of his material culture.

What speculations can we make about the very beginnings of tool manufacture and use? The still very popular myth that depicts the serendipitous discovery by a particularly gifted ape that a naturally flaked stone made a good tool is false on several grounds. First, we know that our remotest tool-using ancestors did not resemble any of the living apes, because these primates are themselves the end products of long and distinct evolutionary lines. Secondly, the extraordinary development of greater intelligence was a slow process in human evolution and was certainly not the initial and decisive factor in tool technology.

Today, we have well-founded evidence to support the view that bipedalism, the ability to walk erect, was the initial determining factor that gave rise to a distinct human evolutionary development among the primates. Bipedalism freed the upper limbs from the necessity of locomotion. Fundamentally, there was now a functional division between the upper and lower limbs. The lower limbs were used solely for locomotion while the upper limbs and hands could be used for gathering and preparing food and for transporting it over longer distances to safer or more convenient storage places, and this with vastly increased efficiency.

Seen in an evolutionary perspective, the use of hands and tools, sticks, bones, and stones, to tear, cut, and to pound and grind foodstuffs is but a simple extension of the functions performed by the jaws.

The development of the human brain, which seems to be correlated with an over-all reduction in the size of the masticatory apparatus, is the result of selective pressures which favored a more effective use of hands and tools to better extract food from the environment.

It would be logical to postulate that man's first step in toolmaking began when he purposedly smashed stones and selected those fragments having a useful cutting edge. But it is obvious that this hypothesis is difficult to verify, for only when such stone fragments are found in association with split and broken bones or other evidence of human activity is it possible to distinguish between stones broken by frost, flowing water or other natural action and stones deliberately broken by man. Moreover, it is probable that this first stage, if indeed it occurred at all, would have been of short duration. It is most likely that these early "ready-made tool" users would have soon discovered that sharp blows with a stone used, for example, to break bones for marrow would remove flakes from the edge of a certain type of stone, and that not only did these flakes have a sharp cutting edge but the edge of the stone used was sharper as well.

It is simply the repetition of this simple gesture of hitting the edge of a stone that formed the basis for the technique of the manufacture of the oldest chopper and flake tools which were first used for long period during the Basal and Lower Pleistocene throughout the three continents of the Old World.

However, not all stones flake in this useful fashion. The first major technological achievement of prehistoric man was the discovery, by experimentation, of all suitable mineral and rock material from which he could shape his implements.

We may now turn our attention briefly to the qualities prehistoric man sought in the various rocks and minerals to be used for tools. There are three: hardness, low tenacity (breakability), and homogeneity. These properties exist in varying degrees in all stones used for the flaking of implements.

The first quality, hardness, is obviously necessary for implements that are used to split, cut, scrape, or grind all kinds of animal or vegetable matter. This led prehistoric man to concentrate chiefly on the siliceous minerals and rocks, by far the hardest of the most common stones. Their major chemical component is quartz (oxide of silicon), the major component of beach sand and one of the hardest of natural substances. On the Mohs scale, which is used to evaluate the hardness of minerals, the siliceous minerals rate number 7, which is surpassed by only a few rarer minerals. They are hard enough to scratch glass (itself number 5½) and can be scratched only by the better qualities of quenched carbon steel, which range between 5 and 8½ on the same scale.

There are no distinctive mineralogical differences between the fine-grained silica minerals; they are only distinguishable on the basis of secondary characteristics such as color, inclusions, or type of geological occurrence. The principal members of the group are chalcedony—which is purest and clearest—and jasper. Both have been used to a limited degree in various parts of the Old World. Flint and chert are the two best-known and most widely used minerals of the group. Chert usually refers to a light-colored variety of flint that occurs in bedded deposits, while flint proper occurs in nodules.

Flint (including chert) was, by far, the material most commonly used in prehistoric Europe and North Africa. It is much less abundant in the rest of the Old World. Rock crystal, another silica mineral occurring in the form of large visible crystals, was used to a limited extent in various parts of the Old World, notably at Chou-kou-tien, in northeastern China.

In addition to the silica minerals, prehistoric man used most of the siliceous rocks. The material most frequently used in Africa, especially south of the Sahara, in China, and in south and southeastern Asia was quartzite, a metamorphic sandstone.

The lack of the better quality siliceous minerals or rocks led Paleolithic man in certain areas to make use of other materials such as fossil wood or certain sedimentary rocks that had been transformed by secondary deposits of silica. Thus, we have collections of prehistoric implements made of silicified volcanic ash or tuff from Burma and Java and of silicified wood from Burma and Eastern Africa. Silicified slate or shale was widely used in South Africa, as well as silcrete, a silicified sandstone.

Although the siliceous stones constituted the major part of the materials used for flaking, other types of stone have been used. Some fine-grained limestones, for instance, have sometimes been flaked for lack of better materials. But more prevalent was the use of slightly softer, but very homogeneous rocks deriving from solidified lava, such as obsidian, basalt, and rhyolite.

Certain types of basalt were flaked in the earliest times in East Africa as well as in India. In volcanic areas, obsidian—the natural glass—was very commonly used for flaking. Prehistoric tools of obsidian are common in the Middle East, a number of Mediterranean islands, Japan, and the Kenya Rift Valley.

The hardness of materials selected for flaking implements would have been of little use to prehistoric man were it not for a second quality these materials held in common to varying degrees, their relatively low tenacity. Tenacity must be distinguished from hardness. Some minerals, such as jade for instance, are not as hard as flint, but are much more difficult to work because of their tenacity or resistance to fracture. Siliceous stones, on the other hand, break rather easily though, of course, they vary considerably in this respect. Flint, for instance, is relatively brittle though it is less brittle than obsidian and much more so than quartzite.

The third quality common to prehistoric stone materials is their mode of fracture which is characteristic of homogeneous materials. Most minerals will fracture along definite plane surfaces that parallel their characteristic crystal symmetry. These natural planes of cleavage limit the number of directions in which a stone can be shaped by flaking. Therefore, prehistoric man tended to select homogeneous materials which have no definite cleavage planes. Such materials are homogeneous either because they lack a well-defined crystal structure (as in the

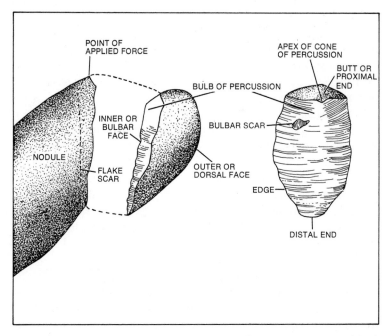

Figure 2. Typical flint flake shown in profile and back view beside the nodule from which it was split. The legend gives the principal terms of knapping nomenclature.

case of the solidified lavas) or because the crystals are minute, as is the case with the majority of the siliceous stones.

A force applied at one point on the surface of such an homogeneous rock or mineral will radiate symmetrically in all directions within a cone whose tip is at the point of impact. This force will punch out a conical fragment having a concentrically rippled surface, leaving a corresponding conical scar in the parent material. If the point of impact is near the edge, a chip will flake off, leaving a rippled half-cone scar. Examples of these two types of scars can frequently be observed on plate-glass counters or windows. Below the point of applied force (see *Figure* 2) is a conical swelling, called the bulb of percussion. It is sometimes accompanied by secondary features such as a bulbar scar due to the flaking of a small chip from its surface. Since the flake's inner surface resembles the surface of a shell, this type of fracture is called a conchoidal fracture—a term derived from the Greek *konchē,* meaning mussel. It is the homogeneity of these materials which make it possible for the knapper to break the stone along planes of fracture whose position can be more or less theoretically determined by manipulative skill alone.

The extent of this skill is quite astonishing, and despite the examination of millions of prehistoric stone implements by archaeologists and extensive experimentation, the full range of the ingenuity and skill of prehistoric stone knappers is yet to be completely shown. Recently, for instance, it was discovered that some prehistoric knappers had probably facilitated the flaking of certain types of siliceous stones by subjecting them to relatively high heat, thereby causing physical changes that are not yet clearly understood.

Figure 3 has been specially prepared to show the diversity and the relations between the various techniques used to apply a flaking force to a stone tool material.

The archaeologist makes a distinction as to whether that force is applied by pressure or by direct or indirect percussion. The degree of the force and the shape, weight, and hardness of the implements used to apply the force are all of great importance, as will be seen later on. The vertical division of *Figure* 3 separates examples of techniques where knapping is achieved by applying a force to a stationary material from those where the material is moved against a stationary object which detaches flakes at the point of contact.

The other variations in manipulative techniques, some of which can be seen in *Figure* 3, pertain first to the manner in which the stone to be flaked is held by the knapper and second to the kind of support used. The main consideration in holding the stone material is the angle at which the stone is held relative to the direction of the force. But there are various ways of holding the stone blank, for instance in the hand, between the knees or feet, or in a clamp, and the various strengths of grip used are also of technical importance.

Finally, important variations exist in the type of support used for the stone material being flaked. Results will depend on whether the hand holding the stone is unsupported, or whether the hand or arm rests or leans against some part of the knapper's body. If an anvil is used to support the stone, the resilience of the anvil's material is also a contributing factor.

The stone knapper's art consisted essentially in the ability to select the most appropriate available material and in developing the manipulative techniques, application of force, type of hold, and type of support which allowed him to shape implements as closely as possible to the forms best suited for the specific tasks for which his stone implements were to be used.

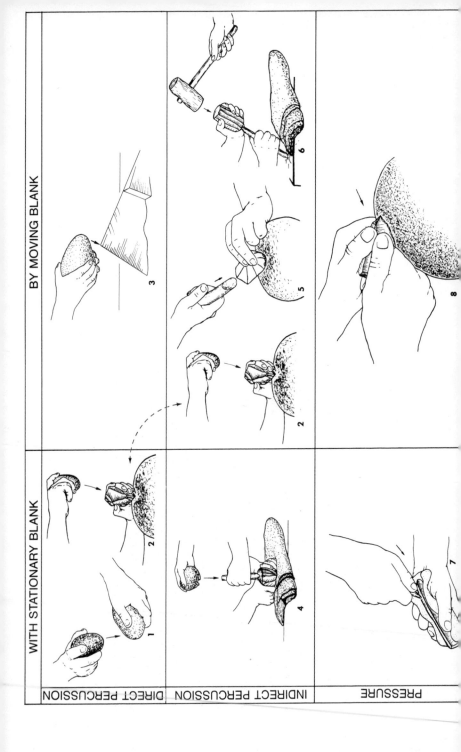

WITH STATIONARY BLANK

BY MOVING BLANK

DIRECT PERCUSSION

INDIRECT PERCUSSION

PRESSURE

Figure 3. Stone-knapping methods. The examples shown are divided horizontally according to the way in which the force is applied (by direct percussion, indirect percussion, and pressure flaking). In-direct percussion usually refers only to the technique shown in 4. How-ever, in the wider meaning used here, it refers to all the methods that combine the strong impetus of a striking hammer (as in direct percussion) with the precision resulting from placing the part of the blank that is to be flaked directly in contact with a flaking device, *retoucheur* or anvil (as in pressure flaking). The left side of the table shows methods by which a moving force removes flakes from a stationary blank. The right side shows examples where the stone to be knapped is moved by percussion or pressure against a sta-tionary object. The bipolar method (2) crosscuts the dividing lines, since it involves a double process in which both the mobile hammer, by direct percussion, and the stationary anvil, by indirect percussion, remove flakes from the blank.

The arrows indicate the general direction of the force used, gen-erally a sort of glancing blow or pressure which, at the same time, compresses and tears away the flake to be removed. The individual components of such a force are indicated on *Figure* 39. A piece of soft material, such as the folded skin (4 and 6), is used to prevent the detached flake from breaking on impact with a hard surface.

III
The Core Tools:
Choppers and Bifaces

There are two basic methods of flaking stone to obtain implements with a useful working edge. With the first method, flakes are removed from a lump of stone—a rounded nodule or large fragment—according to a predetermined design. By analogy with woodwork, the mass of raw material is whittled or trimmed down into the desired shape. Such implements are called core tools, and while the knapper may make use of some of the flakes, they are not his primary interest. His main objective is to obtain a single, massive implement whose cutting edge is formed either by the intersection of two opposite series of flaked scars, or by a series of scars on one side intersecting with the unflaked opposite face of the nodule. The basic aim of the second method is to obtain flakes that may be used either exactly as they come off the nodule, or trimmed (retouched) into specialized tools. In the latter case, the lump of stone is seen essentially as a source of raw material, a nucleus for flakes. It is usually abandoned when suitable flakes can no longer be obtained from it, although there are examples of these exhausted nuclei having been used as heavy scraping tools.

The simplest examples of these two basic methods are already found at the earliest human living floors, those discovered by Dr. and Mrs. L. S. B. Leakey in the Olduvai Gorge, Tanzania. These extraordinary sites, which have yielded both the probable toolmakers and their tools, date to the Late Basal Pleistocene, about one and three quarters million years ago. The remains of man found on these floors have been assigned to two different genera:

Australopithecus boisei (or *Zinjanthropus boisei*) and *Homo habilis*. It is impossible to say whether both genera were the toolmakers, and it has even been suggested that *A. boisei* may have simply been the quarry of *H. habilis*. However, not all anthropologists accept the distinction between the two groups, and the Olduvai hominidae are still referred to as Australopithecines, as are similar fossils from other parts of the Old World. This group is representative of the first stage of human evolution which is characterized by a basically human stance and dentition and a brain of 600 to 700 cubic centimeters, less than half of the present human brain volume.

The majority of the Oldowan tools are simple core tools, called choppers, which measure up to 4 inches in length. They were made by flaking part of the edge of a basalt cobblestone in the manner illustrated in *Figure* 4. Faceted spheroids have also been found; they were made from cobblestones flaked peripherally into a globular shape. Flakes, mainly of quartzite, have also been recovered, most of which show the slightly chipped edges characteristic of use, called by archaeologists use-retouch. Scrapers of various shapes are the most important flake tools. Signs of heavy blows indicating pounding are found on many cobblestones and on the butts of the choppers.

What were these stone choppers used for? No study of their wear pattern is known, but it is likely that they were used both to prepare plant food and for butchering. Many animal bones have been found on the Olduvai Gorge living floors, usually those of small, slow game. But large animals, which had probably either been chased into the nearby lake where they became mired or killed by carnivores and scavenged by these men, were also eaten.

The choppers were probably also used to break open bones for marrow and were perhaps even used occasionally with hammerstones as wedges, judging from the small size of some of the finds. Marrow seems to have been an important food since relatively few unbroken bones have been found, and most of these are scapulae or pelvises, both of which lack marrow.

The faceted spheroids were probably used in the same way as the choppers, although they may well also have been used as missiles—a weapon of great advantage for these early men.

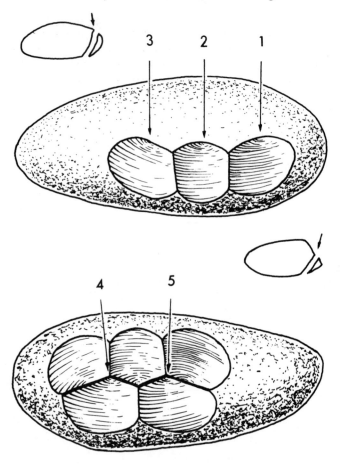

Figure 4. A series of sharp blows (1 through 3) struck near the natural edge of a pebble remove flakes from the under face. The pebble is then turned over, and the next blows (4 and 5) are struck on the ridges formed by the adjacent scars of the first knapping. Result: a chopper tool with a wavy but strong working edge.

These collections of simple core tools and flakes showing little deliberate retouching represent man's most elementary tool kit. This early tool-making tradition, referred to as the Pebble-Tool tradition, or more precisely, as the Chopper and Flake tradition, was used with minor improvements and regional variations over large parts of the Old World for a considerable period of time. Widespread in Africa during the first half of the Lower Pleistocene, the Chopper and Flake tradition is also found at Tell Ubeidiya in the Jordan Valley, and in western Europe at the cave of Vallonet, in southeastern France.

The Chopper and Flake tradition is better demonstrated at a later period, however, in Europe during the second half of the Lower Pleistocene at the site of Vértesszöllös in Hungary. Among other examples of the European Chopper and Flake industries are the collections from Clacton-on-Sea in Essex, England. The Clactonian probably started at the beginning of the Middle Pleistocene or perhaps even a little earlier, lasting until the Riss glaciation at the end of the Middle Pleistocene. Clactonian tools are divided in equal proportions between choppers (including flake cores used as choppers) and flake tools made from thick flakes having a pronounced bulb of percussion and ripples. It is probable that these flakes were obtained by striking the flint nodule first against an anvil (a heavy stone resting on the ground) (see *Figure* 3–3) and then with a heavy hammerstone using the flake scars as successive striking platforms. These flake tools, which are relatively coarsely retouched, include many side-scrapers made by trimming part of the naturally sharp edge of the flake to obtain a more resistant working edge. Other kinds of Clactonian flake tools include notches and denticulates. Notches were made by retouching part of the edge of a flake concavely. They probably served to scrape and shape small cylindrical wooden objects. Quite often these notches were obtained each with a single blow without further retouch at the edge. Denticulates have a series of notches flaked along one edge.

A few backed knives have also been found: these were made by blunting the edge opposite to the cutting edge. They were useful for heavy cutting, since pressure can be applied either with the finger or the palm without injury to the user. Also present in Clactonian collections are *becs*. These are flakes that have been retouched on one edge into a thick point which served as a borer.

In Asia, the tools found at the earliest known sites, Hsi-hou-tu in northeastern China and Kota Tampan in Malaya, probably dating to the middle or early parts of the Lower Pleistocene, also appear to be part of the Chopper and Flake tool tradition. East and Southeast Asia were the most conservative areas of the Old World from the point of view of stone-knapping techniques. The various local industries are grouped into an Asian Chopper-Chopping tool tradition, which essentially corresponds to the Euro-African Chopper and Flake tool technological tradition, grouping the Choukoutienian in China, the Patjitanian in Java, the Anyathian in Burma and the Soan in the Punjab. The Choukoutienian showed the earliest examples of the bipolar knapping method. This method, which was later used in many different areas and periods, was devised to knapp the smaller and rounder stones by placing one of their ends against a hard stone anvil before striking the other end with a hammerstone. In this fashion, stones too small to be conveniently held could be knapped with flakes flying off usually from both ends at the same time (*Figure* 3–2).

The Chopper-Chopping tool tradition lasted at least throughout the entire Middle Pleistocene, a time during which new and very important technological developments in the manufacture of bifaces had long since taken place in Africa and Europe.

Flaking a pebble on two of its opposite edges into a pointed tool—a form prehistorians call a hand-ax, or more generally a biface—was a practice easily derived from the preparation of choppers. In fact, some of the early Chopper and Flake sites found in Africa show a few pebble tools, sometimes called "proto-bifaces," which were flaked in this manner. However, the earliest full-fledged hand-axes are found contemporaneously with evolved examples of Chopper and Flake tools in the Olduvai Gorge and in northwestern Africa, and date to the Lower Pleistocene times. Not much later, hand-axes appeared in northwestern France. The biface tool tradition was to last into the Middle Palaeolithic and to spread over most of the three continents, especially to Africa and western Europe, excluding only the uninhabited northern parts of Europe and Asia, central Asia and Africa, and the conservative Chopper and Flake, or Chopper-Chopping tool areas of eastern and southeastern Asia.

The human remains found at the sites of this period, including those of eastern and southeastern Asia, constitute a morphologically homogeneous group, the Pithecanthropines, whose main characteristic was an increase in cranial capacity to about 1100 cc, or about two thirds the brain volume of modern man.

The new stone tools, the hand-axes, are usually pear-shaped, although their outlines can vary, depending on the period and area of manufacture and the degree of wear, from almost circular to triangular forms. They are flaked over most, if not all, of their edge and usually measure from four to six inches. The majority have a strong, picklike point, as well as a cutting edge, the thickness and curvature of which vary around the periphery of the implement, making it useful for a variety of tasks.

Exactly how were they used? Here again, very few studies of traces of wear have been done. The evidence is against their having been used as missile points; usually they were too bulky and, unless thinned at the base, could not have been securely attached to the spears. Some might have been used as daggers, or wedged into the thick part of wooden clubs as axes, but most of them appear to have been all-purpose hand-held tools for scraping, cutting and chopping. Some were flaked in such a way that the small area which pressed against the palm of the hand was left unchipped; in other cases the user's palm was probably protected either by a pad of animal skin, a mass of resin, or by bark. In general, we may assume that bifaces were used for all heavy chopping, scraping and cutting that could not have been done with the thinner flake tools. Bifaces could also have been used for cutting and roughing out spears or other implements of wood or bark.

The Stone Age technologists progressively improved the effectiveness of the hand-ax. The early types (called Abbevillian in Europe, and Chellean or early Acheulian in Africa) had some serious defects due to the primitive technique used to flake them. When a nodule of flint is flaked by direct hammerstone technique or by hitting it against an anvil, the resulting flakes are short and massive. Their bulbs of percussion leave deep scars, whose intersections form a wavy and inefficient cutting edge. Moreover, since the scars rarely carry very far across the face of the implement, part of the original surface of the nodule remains in the center of the tool, making the

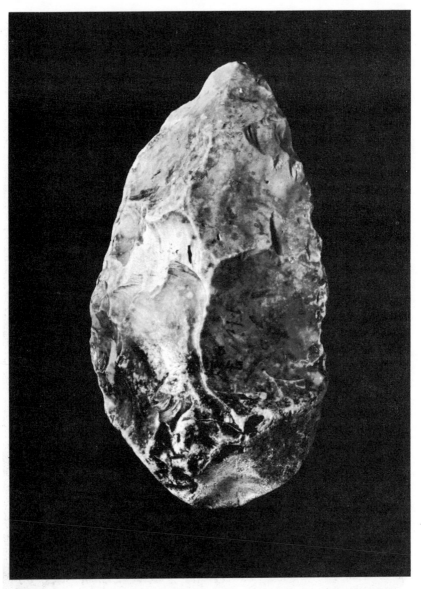

Figure 5. Early core tool, broadside, is a hand-ax that was made by means of Abbevillian technique. Sinuous working edge and deep flake scars are typical of these thick, roughly shaped implements, which apparently were used as all-purpose cutting and chopping tools. The specimen is six inches long and two inches thick.

Figure 6. Side view of hand-ax illustrated in *Figure* 5.

"Abbevillian" hand-ax clumsy because of its thick section (see *Figures* 5 and 6). It is possible, in some cases, to partially straighten the working edge by flaking away the marginal spurs formed by adjacent scars. But this does not give the tool the tapering section necessary for deep chopping or cutting. Experiments have shown that if blows are struck nearer to the flint's edge in an effort to extend the scars across the face, the edge will frequently be crushed. To sum up, then, the "Abbevillian" toolmaker had a mental picture of the reasonably efficient tool he wanted, but his technique was too primitive to allow him to control the shape of his implement in any but a general way. New techniques had to be developed: from them came the Acheulian hand-ax with its straight cutting edge, tapering section and two smooth faces.

The Acheulian knapper used two new techniques for production of his core tools. The first of these was a method of considerable importance, because it was used extensively, in later times, by more advanced makers of stone tools. It consisted of flaking the edge itself, in order to build up preliminary striking platforms set at the correct angle (about perpendicular) to the face to be flaked (see *Figure* 7). The flakes struck from these prepared platforms left scars carrying back across the face of the implement, resulting in a tool with the desired thinner, more tapered section. The preparation of a striking platform,

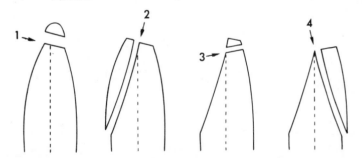

Figure 7. Diagram showing the "turning the edge" technique. First, a part of the nodule's natural edge was struck off, leaving a flat area. The next blow detached a long, shallow flake. A third blow prepared another "platform," and a fourth blow removed a matching shallow flake from the opposite side.

preliminary to flaking, greatly increased the knapper's degree of control over the shape of his bifaces. But most modern experimenters believe that the very shallow flake scars, often with long parallel sides, observed on the Acheulian hand-axes, are possible to produce only by means of an additional trick of technique, probably invented in several different areas at the end of the Lower Pleistocene. This is the baton, or soft-hammer method.

As the name of this second method implies, it involves the use of a hard wood, bone, horn, or antler baton, which, because it is of softer material than stone, can be struck very close to the edge of the nodule without crushing it (see *Figure* 8). In addition, it seems that the use of softer and more elastic hammer material slightly extends the time during which the force acts on the edge of the tool. The flakes resulting from such soft hammer blows—which may sometimes be merely a relatively soft stone—are longer and thinner, have a more diffuse bulb of percussion and flatter ripples than the flakes removed by hard-hammer percussion.

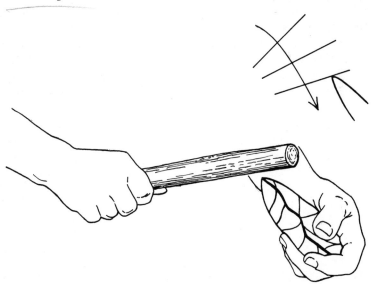

Figure 8. A major advance in biface manufacture was the Acheulian technique of detaching long, shallow flakes with blows of a "baton," striking very close to the tool's edge.

Figure 9. Mid-Acheulian hand-ax, approximately five inches long.

It can be inferred, through examination of the tools and experiments, that the Acheulian hand-axes were first roughed out by hammerstone percussion, with or without preliminary platforms, and then finished with a baton. The Acheulian hand-axes (*Figures* 9 and 10) clearly reveal the characteristic deep, rippled scar resulting from hammerstone percussion, together with the long, shallow scars characteristic of the baton technique. Some of the later Acheulian hand-axes are the most perfect expressions of the core-tool concept (*Figure* 11). Once the knapper had decided on the shape and size best suiting his purpose, he could, by using the platform and baton technique on a rounded nodule or massive flake, produce symmetrically shaped bifaces tapering smoothly toward almost straight edges.

In addition to the hand-ax, the other most characteristic tool in the biface tradition was the cleaver. It first appears in the Olduvai Gorge associated with Acheulian hand-axes dating from the beginning of the Middle Pleistocene. Particularly efficient for skinning and butchering carcasses, as has been demonstrated experimentally, the cleaver has a wide, straight cutting edge perpendicular to the long axis of the tool. This edge is often the preserved natural edge of a large, thick flake that has been bifacially retouched. The cleaver is fairly frequent in western Europe, very common in Africa, and frequent in the rest of the bifacial tool tradition regions such as the Middle East and the Indian continent.

At the better-known European Acheulian sites, the bifacially flaked core tools (used for heavy work) were complemented by a large number of flake tools usually comprising three quarters, and sometimes a little more, of the total number of tools collected (excluding use-retouch flakes). These flake tools were made by retouching biface trimming flakes or flakes that had been obtained in "Clactonian" fashion, that is, by knapping an unprepared nucleus with a stone hammer, or against the edge of an anvil, using the scar of the previously removed flakes as a striking platform. The earliest "Abbevillian" flake tools are little known for few have been collected in undisturbed sites.

The Acheulian flake tools include essentially the same types as previously described for the Clactonian Chopper and Flake collections: side-scrapers, notches, denticulates, backed blades and becs; but the retouch is finer.

Figure 10. Thick lanceolate Acheulian biface. Patination (the white surface at lower right) is due to the weathering of flint by alkaline ground water.

Figure 11. Later core tool shows advanced Acheulian technique: prepared striking platforms, which permitted the knapper to control the implement's shape, and the use of soft hammer percussion for chipping. This triangular Acheulian biface has a thin cross section and straight edges. It is almost six inches long but only three quarters of an inch thick.

Compared to the Acheulian bifacial core tools, which could be shaped quite closely to a predetermined design, the size and shape of the flake tools are quite haphazard since little control could be exercised on the size and shape of the blank flakes.

The making of flake tools, however, has definite advantages over the bifaces. For one thing, their manufacture is not so wasteful of flint as the shaping of a biface which requires the removal of a great deal of material from the flint core, with only a few usable flakes resulting. For another, a flake tool's cutting edge is obtained by a single blow on the flint nucleus, while the production of a similar thin, straight edge by alternate flaking of a biface requires much more time and skill. Finally, the cutting edge of the best possible biface is never so sharp and smooth as that of a flake.

The Acheulian biface makers eventually invented a new way of obtaining tools which combined the basic qualities of core and flake preparation: the Levallois technique to be discussed in the next chapter.

IV
Prepared Flake Nuclei:
Levallois and Mousterian
Flake Tools

An admirable combination of the basic qualities of both core and flake tools was invented by Acheulian biface-makers: the Levallois technique. In this stone-knapping technique, which appeared in several places in Africa and Europe during the Middle Pleistocene (i.e., about 200,000 years ago), the nodule is prepared by careful flaking before the removal of a flake (see *Figure* 12). This preliminary flaking of the outline and top of the nucleus determines a great variety of shapes: pointed, rectangular, oval or even almost circular (see *Figures* 13 through 16). With this method, the size and shape of the tool can be predetermined as in the case of the core tools, and in addition, the knapper can obtain smoothly tapered, very sharp-edged flake tools with ease.

The Levallois technique makes it possible for the knapper to obtain very large flakes. In regions where good stone is comparatively abundant, as in the valleys of northwestern France, it is not unusual to find Levallois points up to six inches long, many of which have been only slightly retouched to obtain a smooth outline. These knappers preferred to make new implements rather than to retouch old tools.

Varieties of the Levallois technique, basically a careful preparation of the nucleus from which the flake tool is removed—a sort of prefabrication—were used extensively by late Acheulian biface-makers in Africa and Europe. These techniques were

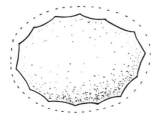

FIRST STEP: trimming edges of nodule.

THIRD STEP: striking platform is made.

Side view of the edge-trimmed nucleus.

Top view of nucleus (*platform, right*).

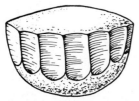

SECOND STEP: top surface is also trimmed.

FINAL STEP: flake struck from nucleus.

Side view of the fully-trimmed nucleus.

Top view of nucleus (*flake is removed*).

Figure 12. The next advance in flint technology was the Levallois technique. By preparing the flint nucleus in advance, a knapper was able to strike off large flakes of predetermined size and shape, which could then serve as implements. Easier to make than a biface, these tools had the advantage of the flake's smooth, sharp edge.

Figure 13. An end product of the Levallois "prepared nucleus" technique is shown in three positions, (*above* and *Figures* 14 and 15). Outer face of the detached flake, *above,* shows the scars of the knapper's preliminary preparation of nucleus (compare *Figure* 12).

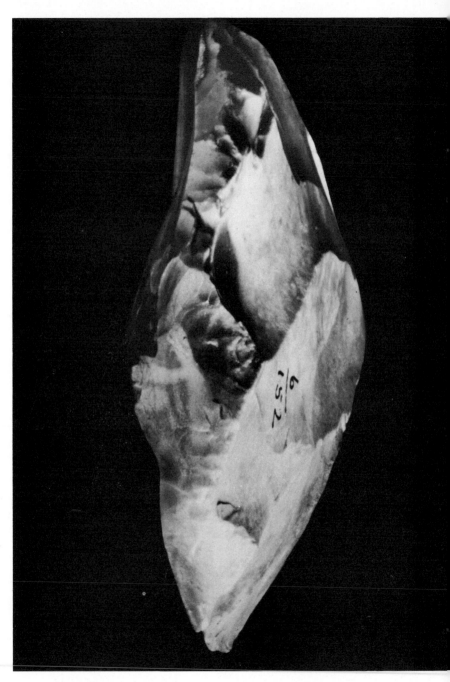

Figure 14. A butt view of the same Levallois flake shows the prepared platform where the knapper struck to detach it.

Figure 15. Smooth bulbar face of the Levallois flake is formed by plane of cleavage from the nucleus. Bulb of percussion can be seen at bottom. Specimen is four inches long.

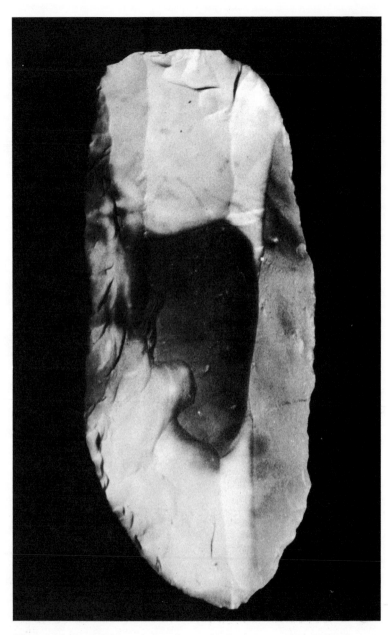

Figure 16. Levallois variation in method of preparing the nucleus is evident from this tool. The knapper first removed several large parallel chips from the top of the nucleus before he detached the blade, five inches long.

to remain in use long after the manufacture of Acheulian bifaces was abandoned by prehistoric man.

The relative proportion of tools in the Acheulian tool kit varies according to the various regions of the Old World. The African Acheulian collections generally include more choppers and faceted spheroids than the west European collections, while flake tools are fewer and less specialized. These differences show the effects of both the diverging customs of relatively isolated groups and the varying human adaptations to different environments.

So few Acheulian living sites are known sufficiently well from the wide range of environments occupied by early man that it is still quite difficult to describe in more than very sketchy terms the way in which the occupants lived.

It is evident, however, that the Acheulian biface-makers were much better equipped than the Chopper and Flake toolmakers, and hunted quite successfully large animals such as elephants, horses, cattle, etc. Plants were naturally also part of their diet. A few depressions—perhaps bedding places—and a few lines of rocks hint at simple dwellings of branches, and perhaps hides weighted by stones.

The command of a better tool kit was the major factor in the spread and successful ecological adaptation of the biface-makers during and after the Mid and Late parts of Lower Pleistocene. Equally, if not more important, however, was the use of fire, first indicated during that period in eastern Asia and western Europe.

The Chou-kou-tien cave deposits in northeastern China, located in the conservative Chopper-Chopping tool province of the Old World, yielded abundant evidence of hearths. Unfortunately the conditions of preservation are not as good for the western European open-air sites, but enough evidence exists to establish that fire was used at the same period: that is, somewhere in the Mid or Late Lower Pleistocene, about 300,000 to 400,000 years ago. In contrast, there is no evidence for the use of fire in Africa before the Mid-Upper Pleistocene as late as 60,000 years ago. Some archaeologists suggest that fire-making techniques were developed long after fire was first used by man. Possibly, at first, man knew only how to keep alive a flame captured from naturally induced fires such as surface fires from oil and shale deposits, forest or prairie fires due to lightning, or even more spectacularly, fires from volcanic eruptions.

There is no archaeological evidence of the first fire-making techniques. These early techniques most probably relied on heat generated by friction, the sawing or the drilling of wood rather than on the sparks obtained by striking a lump of iron pyrite against another or against a piece of flint. Finds of iron pyrites do not occur before the Upper Pleistocene. The earliest evidence for this technique occurs only in Upper Pleistocene sites in Europe.

Once satisfactory techniques for maintaining or making fires had been developed, they provided man with a powerful advantage in his exploitation of nature and permitted him to spread over large territories towards the end of the Middle Pleistocene.

Although the advantages of using fire as protection against the cold, for the preparation of food and as an additional source of light are obvious, fire had another, probably more important use: it served as a powerful repellent to keep predatory animals at a safe distance from the camps. It thus became possible for small bands of men to function in safety, where previously they had been dependent on numerical strength. Man could now range widely and securely in small bands to better exploit plant and animal resources. This led in turn to an increase in population spread over larger territory. In addition, fire probably improved hunting and fishing techniques by being used to attract fish and to gather game.

It was in western Europe and in the Mediterranean lands, at the beginning of the Upper Pleistocene during the Riss-Würm interglacial that the importance of bifacial tools decreased relative to flake tools. This marks the beginning of the Middle Paleolithic period (about 85,000 years ago) which is characterized by the predominance of flake tools. This period lasted until about 35,000 years ago in these regions.

The increased importance of flake tools is probably a consequence of the use of the Levallois technique, which demonstrated the advantages of prepared flake nuclei. The Levallois technique was widely used during the Middle Paleolithic, especially where flint nodules were large, abundant and easily obtained. But there was also another technique of knapping flakes from prepared nuclei which became quite common: the Mousterian discoidal nucleus technique (Le Moustier is a rock shelter in southwestern France) which permitted an extremely efficient and exhaustive flaking of the nucleus.

As in the Levallois technique—to which it is closely related—the nodule of flint was first trimmed peripherally, but instead of trying to get one, or at best two or three flakes of maximum length, the Mousterian knappers concentrated on getting the largest possible number of usable flakes. To achieve this, the nucleus was flaked toward the center from the side scars as for the preparation of the Levallois nucleus, but the flaking was continued until the nucleus was almost completely used up. The flakes obtained were then retouched into specialized tools, usually Mousterian points and scrapers. These were the most common flake tools during the Middle Paleolithic over most of the Old World (see *Figures* 17 and 18).

Mousterian points are flakes that have been retouched into elongated and tapering triangular or oval forms. Scrapers, which are usually the most common stone tool artifact in Mousterian collections, were made by retouching flakes on one or more edges to obtain a thicker working edge. Denticulates, backed knives and other tools, which will be discussed shortly, are found in varying numbers in Mousterian collections, which also occasionally include small hand-axes knapped in the Acheulian fashion.

The names, *points* and *scrapers,* presumably describe the function of these implements. However, the aptness of these terms merits some discussion, and in general, it is important to consider the methods by which the archaeologist attempts to infer the uses to which prehistoric implements were put.

From the definition given for Mousterian points and scrapers, it may have already occurred to the reader that distinguishing points from scrapers can be difficult. If, for instance, the two opposite edges of a scraper have been retouched to converge almost symmetrically into a point at one end, this artifact might well have served as a point. Conversely, an oval point, with a relatively steep retouch might have been used as a double convex scraper.

Figure 17. Flake tool struck from a Mousterian "discoidal nucleus" and retouched to a pointed shape.

Figure 18. Mousterian scraper made from a thick flake of flint by retouching the bottom edge into a steep convex form. Working edges of this sort are strong and this sturdy three-inch-long tool was probably used on wood or on hides.

These difficulties are avoided in archaeological typology since the analysis essentially uses the *formal* attributes of the artifacts only as stylistic indices characteristic of a certain cultural group at a particular time. However, once the geographical and temporal limits of a culture have been established using these attributes, it then becomes desirable to make inferences, where possible, regarding the functions of these tools so that the evolutionary development in the way of life of prehistoric groups can be reconstructed—the ultimate aim of archaeological research.

There are essentially three complementary approaches to the study of the function of prehistoric stone tools. The first, by ethnographic parallels (the observation by ethnologists of the use of similar tools) has always been of primary importance. As we have seen earlier, ethnographic parallels actually demonstrated that the ceraunias were in fact tools and weapons of human fabrication. The second approach is to experimentally test the hypothetical use of a prehistoric tool. This has also been quite useful in several instances, but this technique has not yet been widely employed. The third approach, which is potentially the most important, involves the study of the traces of wear on prehistoric implements. The Russian archaeologist Semenov demonstrated the importance of carefully studying the patterns of striations and polish on the surface of the working edge or on other parts of the tool which were made at the time of its use.

The study of these usually very faint traces is extremely difficult and time-consuming. It requires very careful microscopic examination using light under varied angles of incidence and especially often, the treatment of the surfaces of the tool with colorizers.

Careful studies carried out on complete collections of stone artifacts will eventually yield a solid body of data on the use of prehistoric tools. But, as we have already seen before, too few archaeologists are systematically devoting their time to this type of study, and specific information is still sparse.

In the meantime, we might try also to consider the problem of the function of prehistoric stone tools—in the present occurrence Mousterian tools—by asking what classes of tools prehistoric men might have needed in view of what we already know about their way of life and that of contemporary men at a comparable level of technology.

Basically, man needs four classes of tools.

The first class includes the tools which are moved along the axis of their working edge, that is, longitudinally, and are most frequently maintained in a nearly vertical plane: saws and knives, for instance.

Mousterian denticulate tools, flakes which have a series of small retouched notches along their edges, might have been used for sawing sticks of wood but this is hard to confirm in the absence of wear-pattern studies. Cutting implements, on the other hand, were far more important since they were used very frequently for fundamental tasks such as whittling wood for spear shafts and for probably many other wooden implements which have not survived.

Cutting implements were also necessary to skin, dismember, and parcel carcasses, and to cut meat at the time it was eaten. Since the most efficient cutting edges are the natural edges of the flakes just removed from the nucleus, it is likely that a large number of the unretouched flakes commonly found at a site, that were large enough to be held between the fingers, were casually used as knives and thrown away after they had served their purpose. Also used as knives were flakes that had been only lightly retouched, probably to smooth out the cutting edge or to provide a place on the opposite edge where the fingers could be placed to exert greater pressure on the flake knife. Backed knives, which are found in some Mousterian and Acheulian collections, are long, narrow flakes which have been abruptly retouched on one edge for the same purpose.

The second class of tools includes those which are used by moving them perpendicularly to the axis of their working edges, that is, transversely, and usually in a nearly horizontal plane. Examples include such tools as gouges, chisels, and scrapers, and the modern planes. Retouching a scraper in effect dulls the naturally sharp cutting edge of the flake. This is an advantage when dressing pelts, for instance, since the tool does not then tear the skin. The retouch also makes the edge thicker and more resistant which is necessary for working wood.

Mousterian scrapers come in many shapes and are usually two to three inches long (see *Figure* 18). Convex-edged scrapers particularly, and straight-edged as well, were probably used to work skins and wood and are the most common type of Mousterian scrapers. Concave scrapers were also made, though less frequently, and they were probably used as spokeshaves to work sticks into hafts and the like.

The third main class of tools is basic to any process of manufacturing: it is the class of tools used to perforate. In this class are included the borers found with relative frequency in Mousterian collections. They are flakes having a short and thick bifacially retouched point projecting from one edge. Borers were probably used to make holes in wood. We should ask whether Mousterian points should also be included in the class of perforating implements. While it is possible that a few of the thinner and more symmetrical points may have been attached to spears or javelins, most of the Mousterian points, which in any case would have been relatively difficult to haft, would be too thick to penetrate the hides of animals such as the woolly rhinoceros, mammoth and bear which were hunted in those times. On the other hand, the use of fire-hardened, pointed, wooden spears, already known from the Lower Paleolithic, would have been a far more reliable method for killing these animals. It seems likely, therefore, that the majority of the Mousterian points, which usually measure two to three inches, were more probably used as pointed cutting and scraping implements.

With the exception of the hypothetical spear or javelin stone points, all of the implements just discussed were used by applying the force needed when the tool was already in contact with the material being worked.

In the fourth and last class of tools are included the percussive tools. Hammerstones for flaking flint or pounding various types of materials are typical examples. Some of the Mousterian choppers, hand-axes and cleavers for instance might also have been used in this fashion, for some of the phases of the butchering of a carcass, or perhaps for chopping wood. There is no evidence that the Mousterian hand-axes or cleavers were hafted, but the thinner ones might well have been set in a hole or slot made in a wooden handle and used as a weapon or a chopping tool. The last example serves to remind us that, within limits, tools can be used for diverse purposes and it is often difficult to distinguish between them. A Mousterian point, for instance, could have been used as a spear tip but it could just as well been used as a knife, which itself could have been used either as a cutting implement or for light scraping, depending on the needs or preferences of its owner.

Conversely, archaeological typologies often make a distinction between certain types of tools which might well have been used for the same purpose. Thus without experimentation and detailed studies of wear patterns, which have yet to be made, it would be specious to see in the dozens of types of Mousterian scrapers, distinguished by name, the same number of different tools each made for a specific purpose. Functional classification will probably cut across the traditional classifications of prehistoric tools which have been based mainly on over-all shape.

The difficulties inherent in the functional study of prehistoric implements are further increased by the fact that the collections usually studied by archaeologists are not entirely representative of the activities of the groups that lived on prehistoric sites.

First, one should recognize that many of the implements collected from archaeological sites are actually worn-out tools that had probably been retouched several times during the course of their useful life, not only to repair damaged edges, but sometimes to transform the tool to suit another purpose as well. For instance, a Mousterian point whose edges had been dulled or chipped in the course of its use as a knife could be retouched to make a double scraper. Similarly, a convex scraper might have been retouched into a straight or concave scraper before being discarded. This parsimony was particularly prevalent when flint was relatively rare, and the abandoned tools recovered by the archaeologist would, therefore, not be truly representative of the complete range of activities carried on by a group of prehistoric people.

Second, archaeologists have traditionally concentrated on specialized tools such as points, scrapers, etc., because they offer many specific varieties of shape and types of retouch useful in the study of the temporal and geographical distribution of the various prehistoric groups. In reality, these specialized tools usually represent the lesser part of the total number of chipped stone implements found in archaeological layers. The other part, which usually represents from 50 to 90 per cent of the total specimens, includes the unretouched chips and flakes. Often referred to as *débitage,* or waste, the assumption usually made is that unretouched chips and flakes are the discarded waste from the manufacture of the "proper" tools, that is, the traditionally recognized specialized tools. Actually, many of these unretouched flakes were probably used.

Ethnographic field observations of the Australian aborigines, for instance, very clearly indicate that, in general, tools are retouched only when absolutely necessary and that any available flake is used for ordinary jobs and then thrown away when no longer needed. Most of these "casual" tools have no grossly apparent signs of repeated use such as nicked edges.

It seems reasonable to assume that the "law of least effort" was as valid in prehistoric times as it is today and that the most frequent technical activity, cutting, was probably most often done with unworked stone flakes and chips; precisely those chips and flakes which most archaeologists have in the past, at best, merely counted and put aside during the study of collections. On the basis of ethnographic evidence it would appear that such material should also be taken into consideration if a more faithful picture of the activities of prehistoric man is to be obtained.

Thus it is evident that the analysis of the functions of prehistoric stone tools poses many difficulties. At present, many current inferences are still too hypothetical and too general to be of real use. Systematic studies of traces of wear on collections of all of the chipped stone specimens from undisturbed archaeological layers are necessary before more progress can be made in this important field.

Before resuming our discussion of the Middle Paleolithic tools, it might be useful to deal with a question that may have occurred to the reader: why would prehistoric man have gone to the trouble of retouching flakes into conventional, specialized shapes if he could accomplish so much with unretouched flakes?

There are two major reasons. The first is a technical one. Retouched specialized tools are necessary for finer work such as scraping very resistant material, making neat grooves in wood, or cutting with great precision.

The second reason for retouching flakes might be more important than it appears at first sight: the pride a person feels in using, and *a fortiori* making, a good tool manufactured according to the standards of the social group of which he is a part.

It is difficult, for instance, to attribute distinct functions to each of the dozen basic shapes of Acheulian bifaces recognized by archaeologists. The various prehistoric groups used some of these preferentially not so much because they were better adapted to specific tasks, which were fundamentally the same during any period, but more probably because they were fashionable during certain periods in certain areas.

Similarly, it might be suggested that even though almost any type of unretouched flake could be used more or less efficiently to butcher or to work wood or hide, for instance, there were cultural standards, probably more important for some people than for others in any one group, which favored the use of the "proper" tool. A modern analogy might be that in some present-day households, kitchen knives are used for all sorts of tasks for which they were not specifically designed (opening jars or cans, for example), while in other households such behavior would be strongly opposed and only the proper tool, available and well cared for, would be used.

The Middle Paleolithic flake tools represent a significant progress in stone technology. To be sure, flake edges had often been retouched by earlier prehistoric man for tasks which could not be done conveniently with bifaces. But these rather haphazard early flake tools are much inferior to the Middle Paleolithic tools which are of predetermined design and show greater diversification and specialization.

In contrast with this richer chipped stone industry, the use of bone and antler did not progress much in the Middle Paleolithic. Butchering marks are sometimes found on bones, but there are only a few examples of bones actually worked into tools. Faint traces of wear (probably often missed on such specimens) have been found on bone splinters which were apparently used as awls or possibly spear points. A few bone specimens appear to have been used either as anvils on which to rest flint; or perhaps as knapping hammers. Antler was sawed into pieces, but there are few clues as to its use.

Though the only wooden implement recovered from the Middle Paleolithic is the Lehringen spear mentioned earlier, the number and variety of the Mousterian manufacturing stone tools suggest that wood, which is easier to work than bone or antler, was frequently used to make hafts, handles, posts, and other objects of common use. A few years ago, at Combe-Grenal, a Mousterian site in Dordogne, southwestern France, Professor Bordes was able to make a cast of a hole left by a wooden picket long disappeared since it may have helped to hold up a shelter made out of skins or branches.

It was apparently during the Middle Paleolithic that the first examples of stone artifacts shaped by pecking the surface with hammerstones made their appearance. Among these are small grinders for pigments which were probably used to decorate the skin or artifacts, since wall paintings are not known from this period. Other pecked stone artifacts relatively common from this period are spherical stone balls. They are generally found in groups of three and might have been tied together like the

Argentinian bolas and hurled at the quarry to entangle its feet during the hunt.

As a whole, the Middle Paleolithic technology suggests a greater efficiency in the exploitation of the environment as is evidenced by the spread of the Mousterian sites in the Old World, especially in the relatively colder and damper regions of northern Europe during the first part of the Würm glaciation.

The heartland of the Mousterian is Europe, the Middle East and North Africa. But "Mousteroid" flake tool industries usually assimilated to the Mousterian exist also in China, perhaps India, and also in Africa, south of the Sahara where they apparently began and ended later than the Mousterian proper in the northern hemisphere.

Who occupied the Mousterian sites? The human remains found associated with Mousterian or Mousterian-like industries in various parts of the Old World are usually grouped together as Neanderthals or Neanderthaloids. From their Pithecanthropine forebears, they seem to have retained the massive skeleton and dentition, flat forehead, and heavy brow ridges. Their skull, however, is more voluminous, especially posteriorly, and contained a brain of about 1500 cc., which is equal to or even somewhat greater than the average brain capacity of man today.

Neanderthals often lived in caves or rock shelters which protected them from the elements. In some instances, remains of stone paving and post holes indicate that they sometimes built rough constructions, probably of skins or branches, held up by rows of posts set near the entrance to a cave. But open-air sites are quite common; the summers must have been relatively warm in the middle northern latitudes. The open-air sites sometimes show rings of debris pushed into rough circles probably serving as walls to support roofs made of skins or branches.

One of the most interesting of these Mousterian sites is Molodova, in Soviet Moldavia, where a hut was found with a wall made of skulls, shoulder blades, tusks, and bones of mammoths. It enclosed an area approximately 20 by 26 feet containing the remains of fifteen small hearths.

It is also from the Neanderthals that we have the first evidence of aesthetic considerations divorced from functional ones.

At Arcy-sur-Cure, 100 miles southeast of Paris, Professor Leroi-Gourhan found a few objects in Mousterian layers that had apparently been collected by Neanderthals as curiosities: the fossil cast of a gastropod shell, a spherical polypide, and a few nodules of iron pyrite stuck together.

Tata, a Mousterian site in Hungary, yielded incised pebbles and an oval piece of mammoth ivory covered with ochre pigments.

Pieces of ochre and lumps of black manganese dioxide, probably used for skin decoration, are actually quite common in Mousterian sites. Of particular interest have also been the cave burials of flexed bodies, sometimes covered with stones, the first available evidence for funerary practices.

V
The Blade Tools

A few decades ago, prehistorians saw little continuity between the Middle and the Upper Paleolithic. The Neanderthals were believed to have been suddenly replaced by invading groups of modern men with a totally different culture.

The differences were striking. The stone tool collections from the Upper Paleolithic sites showed much greater variations between sites and included many more types of tools. Many of these sites also yielded many different kinds of bone and antler implements often decorated by incision and modelling. Burials with ochre and body ornaments of perforated shells and animal teeth, as well as the cave paintings, engravings and reliefs indicated artistic and religious concerns on an entirely new scale.

However, as research progressed, it became evident that the significance of the morphological differences between the Neanderthals and modern men had been over-emphasized. Human fossils with intermediate characteristics were found. Today, it seems more likely that the direct ancestors of modern men may be related to some Neanderthal populations. Recent archaeological studies indicated similarly that the extent of the gap between Middle and Upper Paleolithic industries had been exaggerated. A number of Upper Paleolithic stone tools have their roots in the Middle Paleolithic and it now seems probable that Upper Paleolithic industries evolved from the Mousterian flake industries in several areas of the Old World. In Europe where this transition is relatively better known and perhaps the earliest, it is estimated to have taken place between 35,000 and 40,000 years ago.

The most striking feature of the Upper Paleolithic industries is the increase in types of specialized stone blade tools. Most of the Mousterian flake tools can still be found in many Upper Paleolithic collections, but one finds in addition a considerable increase in the number of specialized tools made from long and relatively thin flakes with parallel sides, called blades which are at least twice as long as they are wide (see *Figure* 19). Shorter and narrower blades measuring less than two inches by one half inch are usually called bladelets. Blades and more rarely bladelets were made in earlier times, notably in the Middle Paleolithic, when they were sometimes obtained from prepared blade nuclei, in a manner similar to those made in the Upper Paleolithic. However, these blade and bladelets become particularly numerous in the Upper Paleolithic, while they only occur occasionally in earlier collections.

Ideally, the simplest way to prepare a blade nucleus is to first break the end of a flint nodule perpendicular to its long axis, and then, using the plane of segmentation as a striking platform, carefully trim the surface of the nodule with a hammerstone into a roughly pyramidal or cylindrical shape (see *Figure* 20). The blades are then detached by a series of blows struck along a spiral line, starting at a point near the edge of the striking platform and finishing almost at its center. By analogy, this knapping process resembles the careful unwinding and sectioning of a rolled sheet of material (see *Figure* 20–8). In practice, it is relatively rare to find Upper Paleolithic blade nuclei that come close to the theoretical shape of *Figure* 20. On most of the nuclei, blades are shown to have been removed in series, but these are frequently interrupted by irregularities in the stone or accidents in the knapping process (see *Figure* 21).

There is evidence on some blade nuclei to suggest that the knapper will prepare for the removal of the first blade by first flaking a vertical ridge along the side of the trimmed nucleus. A blow struck just above this projection will remove a ridged or crested blade—*lame à crête*—which shows on its dorsal face the ridge scars of the preparatory flaking (see *Figure* 20–1). The removal of the ridged blade will leave a vertical scar with two parallel ridges which can be used as a guide for the removal of the following blade. If the blade is struck from the striking platform between two ridges, the butt and the blade section will

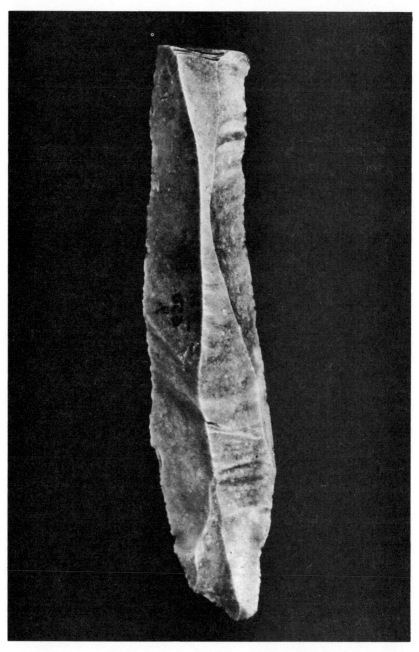

Figure 19. Blades of this type are the "raw materials" from which, by means of subsequent retouching, the knappers of the Upper Paleolithic made most of their specialized stone tools. The blade, under four inches, is only a quarter-inch in thickness.

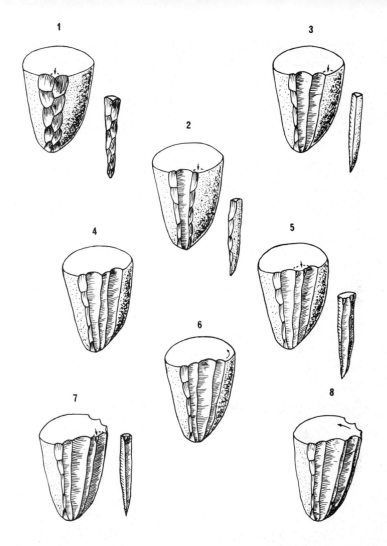

Figure 20. Knapping of blade or bladelet nucleus. A vertical ridge
is flaked along the side of the nodule. The crested blade (1) removed
by a blow on the broken end of the nodule serving as the striking
platform leaves parallel ridges guiding the knapping of the following
blades (2 and 3). The overhang and spurs formed on the edge of
the nucleus by deep bulbar scars left by the first series of blades
are chipped away before a new series is removed (5 and 7). The
arrows in 6 and 8 show the progression of knapping which "un-
wraps" the blade nucleus. Note that the section of the removed
blades (5 and 7) depends on the place where the knapping force is
applied: it will be trapezoidal when the force is applied between
two vertical ridges (5), triangular when it is applied just above one
vertical ridge (7).

Figure 21. Side view of a four-and-a-half-inch-long blade nucleus.

be trapezoidal (*Figure* 20–5). If it has been stuck just above one of the ridges, the butt and cross section will be triangular (see *Figure* 20–7).

The majority of archaeologists today believe that most of the Upper Paleolithic blade nuclei were knapped by the indirect percussion method illustrated in *Figure* 3–4.

This method involves the use of an intermediate tool, a punch, which is placed between the hammer and the striking platform of the nucleus. The advantage of this method is that the force of the hammer, made of stone, bone, antler, or wood, can be directed very precisely to a point on the striking platform of the nucleus through the use of the punch. The knapping of the nuclei can thus be accomplished with more precision than would be possible with the method of direct percussion by striking the platform directly with a hammer.

Because the punch is usually held at an angle to the striking platform, its tip is likely to slip on the surface of the nucleus when the hammer blow is struck. One can sometimes see that the knappers tried to prevent this by delicately flaking the edge of the platform to provide a seat for the tip of the punch.

Indirect percussion seems to produce blades with a relatively thick bulb of percussion. The resulting deep bulbar scars form a fragile overhang at the edge of the platform with spurs at the edges of the blade scars. The knapper must usually flake off these spurs to facilitate the removal of new blades nearer the center of the nucleus.

Blades have also been knapped experimentally by the direct percussion method using a hand stone hammer or softer hammers made of antler. Stone hammers have been recovered in archaeological layers but in surprisingly low numbers even in flint-knapping sites which have been very carefully excavated. However, none of the hypothetical punches seen have been identified although many other implements made of bone and antler, the material one would think most appropriate for such tools, have been preserved from the Upper Paleolithic. It is possible, of course, that the punches were made exclusively of hard wood and have since decayed. But it is also possible that the direct stone percussion method was much more prevalent than is now believed. If this is the case, the question still remains as to why so few hammerstones have been found. This, however, might be easier to explain than having to assume that all punches were made of wood and that they have all vanished. We might consider, for instance, the possibility that flint knapping had long since reached a level of complexity and skill which could not be mastered by every man.

In this case, some men would have been more dextrous than others and might well have been given the task, whenever possible, of flaking flint nuclei because they were the most proficient among a particular group of families living together. Moreover, for the flint knapper of prehistoric times as well as today, good hammerstones—that is stones of proper density and shape—are extremely valuable tools which are used until they eventually break with an ill-placed blow. Perhaps the reason why so few hammerstones have been found is because knappers represented a relatively small group and that they would rarely have abandoned serviceable hammerstones. Rather, they would have kept these valuable tools, packing them along with their other possessions during the seasonal moves of the band from camp to camp.

With the prevailing use of blades there is a marked diminution of the dimensions of stone tool implements compared to the earlier ones. This is why the Upper Paleolithic has sometimes also been referred to as the Leptolithic, from the Greek, meaning lighter stone.

The trend toward lighter implements was constant during the Paleolithic since the first choppers and Abbevillian bifaces were manufactured and it continued, as we shall see later, during the Mesolithic with the manufacture of very small bladelets and microlithic tools. The development of techniques which allow the knapper to prepare smaller tools tends to increase the efficiency of flint knapping, since more usable edge can be obtained for a given amount of flint. Professor Leroi-Gourhan of the Sorbonne, for instance, calculated that the Acheulian technique of biface preparation approximately tripled the amount of usable edge that could be obtained from a nodule of flint since the knapper could flake several thinner bifaces instead of one chopper or Abbevillian biface.

The preparation of Levallois and Mousterian flake nuclei

increases by about four times the amount of edge obtainable with the Clactonian flaking technique. With the blade nuclei technique the progress is even greater. A knapper could flake a much larger amount of blades and bladelets representing, for the same amount of flint, up to five times the length of working edge represented by the Levallois and Mousterian flakes.

The development of knapping techniques which increased the ratio of the length of usable edge for a given quantity of flint must have been important to prehistoric man. Hunters and gatherers can only carry a limited amount of material with them during their seasonal migrations and hunting expeditions. With more efficient methods of knapping flint, their range could be extended farther and for longer periods of time into areas where flint was locally unavailable, of poorer quality, or difficult in access.

The progress in knapping techniques during the Upper Paleolithic represented by the prepared blade nuclei was accompanied by an increase in the number of different types of tools. During the Middle Paleolithic, the number of flake tools had already increased relatively to the earlier period where a few specialized flake tools accompanied the bifaces, which were essentially all-purpose tools.

During the Upper Paleolithic, there was an even greater variety of tools made from retouched blades intended for some specific tasks.

The most common blade tools of the European Upper Paleolithic, which will now be described, are backed blades, end-scrapers, and burins. Large but thin bifacial points or knives made from blades were also common, especially in eastern and central Europe.

Backed blades are blades with an edge that has been purposely blunted by abrupt percussion retouch, (*Figure* 22–1, 2, 4). Experiments have shown that an animal can be skinned with a backed blade almost as rapidly as with a steel knife, by applying pressure with the index finger on the blunted edge. Steep retouch of this kind was also done occasionally across the width of the blade. This truncation, which is the technical term for a transversal abrupt retouch, is very convenient for applying pressure with the thumb of the left hand to increase the cutting or scraping action of the working edge of the blade held between the fingers of the right hand. In some cases, the backing has

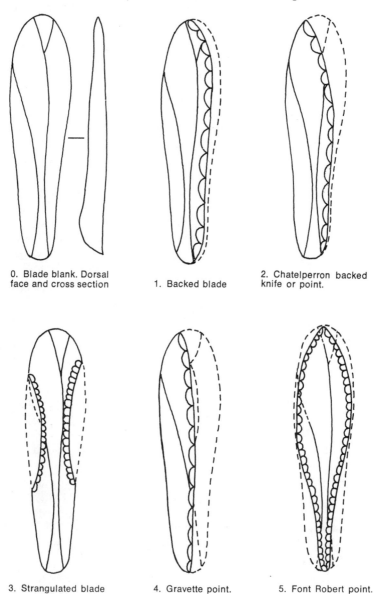

0. Blade blank. Dorsal face and cross section

1. Backed blade

2. Chatelperron backed knife or point.

3. Strangulated blade

4. Gravette point.

5. Font Robert point.

Figure 22. Schematic drawings of retouched Upper Paleolithic tools superimposed over a blade or bladelet blank. Lower end is the proximal end with the bulb of percussion shown once in cross section.

6. Noailles burin.

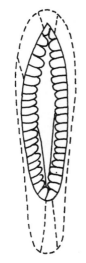

7. Solutrean unifacial point.

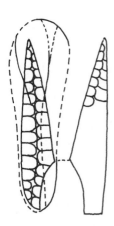

8. Shouldered point.

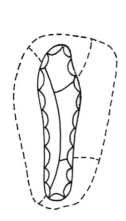

9. Raclette.

10. Parrot beak burin.

11. Teyjat point.

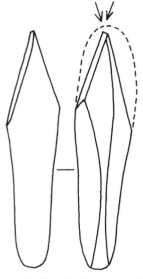

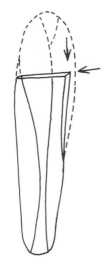

12. Straight dihedral burin.

13. Canted dihedral burin.

14. Angular dihedral burin.

15. Multiple dihedral burin.

16. Busqued burin.

17. Burin on straight truncation.

18. Burin on oblique truncation.

19. Multiple burin on double truncations.

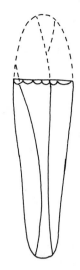

20. Blade with straight truncation.

21. Blade with oblique truncation.

22. Blade with two oblique truncations.

23. End-scraper.

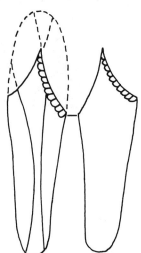

24. Double end-scraper.

25. Straight borer with alternate bilateral retouch.

26. Canted borer with bilateral unifacial retouch.

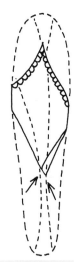

27. End-scraper/burin (straight dihedral).

28. End-scraper/borer.

29. Borer burin (straight dihedral).

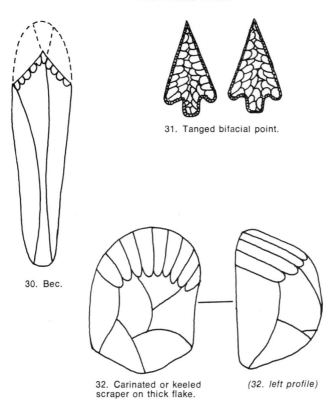

30. Bec.

31. Tanged bifacial point.

32. Carinated or keeled scraper on thick flake.

(32. left profile)

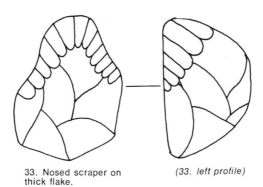

33. Nosed scraper on thick flake.

(33. left profile)

34. Bladelet blank. Dorsal face and cross section.

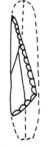

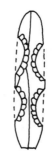

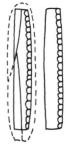

35. Triangle bladelet.

36. Rectangle bladelet.

37. Bilaterally denticulated bladelet.

38. Dufour bladelet alternately retouched on opposite sides.

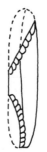

39. Magdalenian shouldered point.

been done in such a way as to form a strong trihedral point with the opposite edge at one end of the blade (*Figure* 23). It is quite likely that this sort of backed point was used as a tip or to form a cutting edge on the side of a spear.

End-scrapers are blades whose ends have been retouched into a rounded scraping edge (*Figures* 22–23; 24 and 25). The sides of such tools might also have served as cutting edges. End-scrapers, as well as other blade tools, can be used by simply holding them between the fingers, or perhaps as a precautionary measure, in a fold of leather to prevent the user from cutting himself. Another method, still used by Australian aborigines, consists of inserting the proximal end of the stone tools into a small mass of heated resin which itself serves as a handle.

Very few handles of any kind have yet been found in Paleolithic sites. But it is evident, at least for the Upper Paleolithic, that hafting was common since we have many tanged stone points from this period, and also bone points made with beveled, split, or tanged bases which could not have been used otherwise. On the basis of handles found in later periods (see *Figure* 26), and from ethnographic evidence, archaeologists have suggested that the specialized tools might also have been hafted into split or grooved handles of wood, antler, or bone and held there with resin. Too few studies have yet been made on traces of wear and areas of use retouch which might indicate the use of a handle and its approximate shape. But it is likely that practices varied greatly depending on the task to be done, and the availability of raw materials.

One of the most important technological developments of the Upper Paleolithic was the manufacture of a large number of bone and antler implements such as spear and harpoon points.

Some artifacts made of these materials have been recovered from sites of the Middle and even the Lower Paleolithic periods, but they are usually only very roughly shaped. This was probably done according to some evidence by first chopping the material into pieces of an appropriate size, and then roughly shaping it by alternately charring and scraping its surface. According to ethnographic evidence, this method is widely used to shape wood and it is most probably of very great antiquity for working wood, bone and antler.

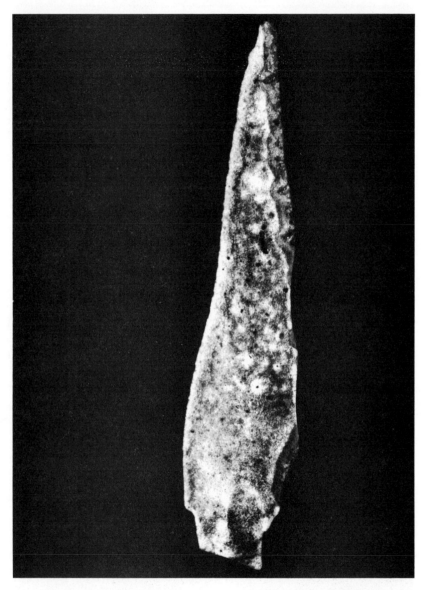

Figure 23. A hypothetical "tool kit" of the Upper Paleolithic period (*Figures* 23 through 33) has been assembled from sites of varying cultures and dates. All of the tools, except for the heavy-duty scraper (*Figure* 29) were made from blades. The Gravette point, *above,* could have been used as a knife or may have been side-hafted as the blade of a spear. All implements shown are between two and three and one half inches except for those reproduced in Figures 24 and 26 (*top*).

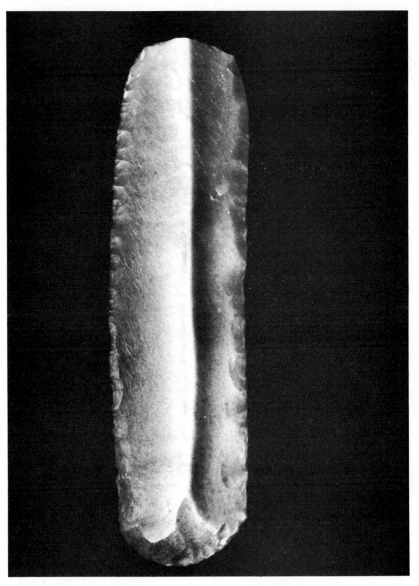

Figure 24. An end-scraper on a blade four inches long.

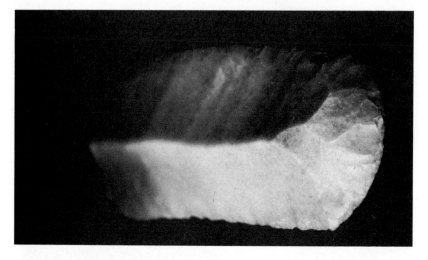

Figure 25. Working end of end-scraper shown in *Figure* 24.

It was the development of the burin during the Upper Paleo-lithic that made possible the manufacture of finely shaped imple-ments of bone, antler, and ivory. The retouched edge of a scraper is stronger than the thin edge of an unretouched blade of flake, but it does not have the proper chisel edge, peculiar to the burin, which is necessary to carve these hard materials efficiently and *a fortiori* to make even easier the working of wood (*Figures* 27 and 28). Burins are sometimes found in Middle and even Lower Paleolithic sites, but it is only during the Upper Paleolithic period that they were produced in great numbers and variety.

Archaeologists recognize two main varieties of burins accord-ing to the shapes of the working edge. These shapes depend on the use for which the burin was intended by its maker, the number of reflakings of the worn edges, and the traditions of the various groups of men.

The first step in manufacturing a burin is the truncation of a blade perpendicularly or obliquely to its long axis to obtain a perpendicular edge at one end across the width of the blade. This can be achieved either by snapping the end of the blade

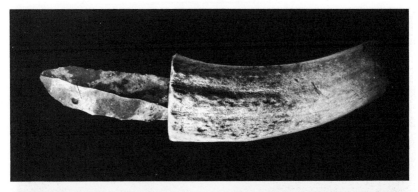

Figure 26. Hafted blade tools. These knives are from Swiss Neolithic sites, but it is probable that some tools were set in similar fashion in wood, bone, or antler by Paleolithic artisans. The implement shown on top is almost six inches long; the one shown below is three and one half inches.

or by retouching it abruptly at one end (*Figure* 22–20, 21, 22). One corner of the truncated end is then removed using the truncated end as a striking platform leaving one or several long, thin triangular facets. The chisel edge of the burin is formed by the intersection of the truncated end with the faceted edge. This type

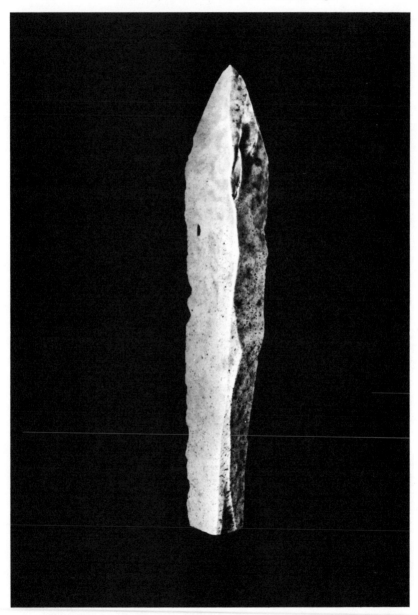

Figure 27. Straight dihedral burin.

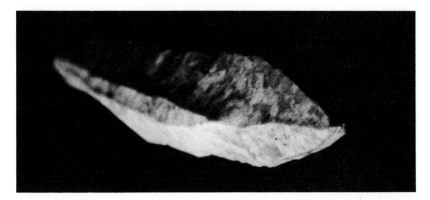

Figure 28. Working end of dihedral burin shown in *Figure* 27.

of burin is called "burin on retouched truncation" (*Figure* 22–6, 10, 17, 18, 19). The knapper may also use the upper corner of the triangular facet as a striking platform for one or several blows removing the entire truncated end leaving another faceted edge. The chisel edge of the burin is formed, in this case, by the intersection of the two faceted edges (*Figure* 22–12 to 15). These burins are called "dihedral burins."

Burins were apparently used both to make rough blanks of bone, antler, and ivory, and to finish them into tools. The older fragmentation methods, that is, the percussion, charring, and scraping methods, continued to be used to obtain sections of these materials, but it is probable that the burin was used to carve deep circular grooves in the relatively hard surface of antler, bone or tusks making it possible to break them neatly by percussion at the places weakened by the carving of the grooves.

Rough blanks for tools were probably obtained from these fragments in two ways. The first involves the splitting of a length of the material by using wedges hammered into slots. In the second, called the groove and splinter method, burins were used to carve parallel grooves which isolated slivers of material that could be pried off once the underlying spongy tissue of the bone or antler was reached. These slivers were

then finished by carving and by scraping for which the thick
perpendicular side edge of the burins was used, and finally,
abrasive stone was used to grind the slivers into the desired
forms.

These implements, which were often decorated with burin in-
cisions, include spear points with split, beveled, or tanged bases
for hafting; harpoon heads with a single or double row of barbs;
awls, needles, and other articles such as polishers and spear
throwers.

It is well known from ethnological sources and experiments
that wetting and steaming bone, antler, and ivory will make
these materials easier to work by softening them temporarily.
Steaming can also be used to straighten, when necessary, the
natural curve of these materials, and it is probable that such
techniques were used by Upper Paleolithic man.

The presence of backed blades, end-scrapers, and burins in
large number and variety, too numerous to be further described
here, is characteristic of the Upper Paleolithic collections. It is
similarly impossible to describe here the many other tools used
such as truncated blades, denticulated and notched blades, the
various types of borers, the many different kinds of projectile
points, and the keeled or nosed scrapers made on heavy flakes.
Figure 22 consists of schematic drawings of some of these types
of tools found in the Périgord in southwestern France, the richest
area in prehistoric remains in Western Europe. For photographs
of Upper Paleolithic tools, see *Figures* 23 to 38.

Most of these tools were common to prehistoric man over
the greater part of Europe, including Russia, the Middle East,
and North Africa, although the relative importance of the various
types within each tool kit varies according to time and place.
The types of tools manufactured from region to region show
little over-all contrast. It might be said, however, that as a
whole the Upper Paleolithic in France is characterized by the
relatively large number of multiple tools, that is, blades which
are worked at both ends either into the same tools, such as
double end-scrapers or double borers (*Figure* 22–6, 15, 19, 24)
or worked into different tools, such as those having a burin at
one end and a scraper at the other (*Figure* 22–27, 28, 29, 32,
and 33).

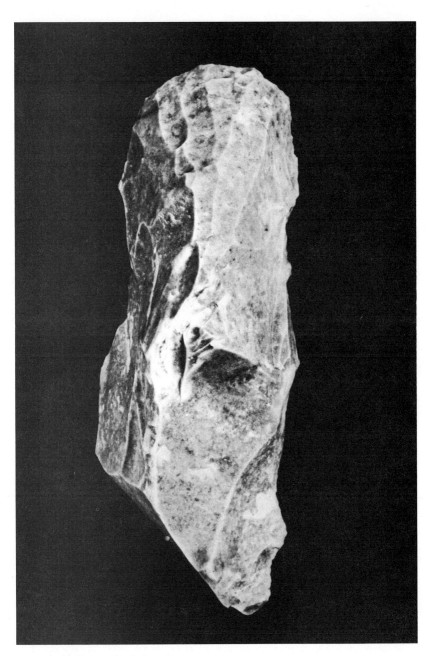

Figure 29. Heavy keeled scraper.

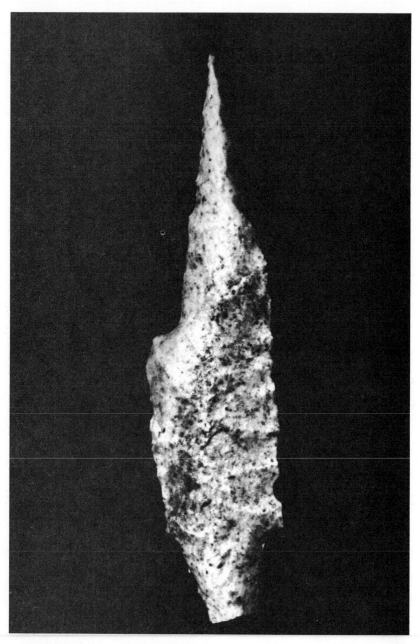

Figure 30. Solutrean double perforator (broken).

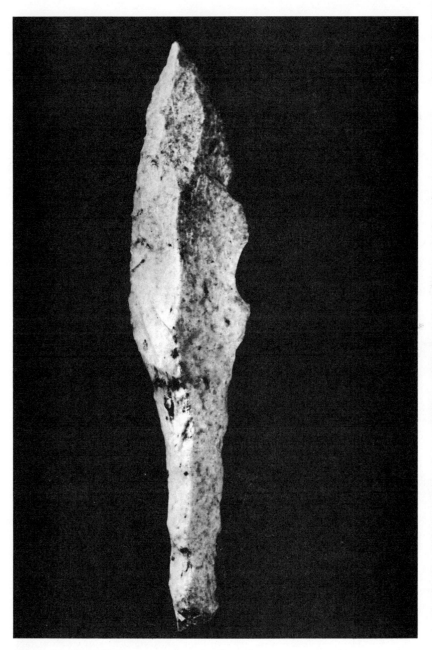

Figure 31. Font Robert tanged projectile point.

In the same general terms, eastern and central Europe, in contrast, are distinguished by the presence, in the earliest Upper Paleolithic sites, of large (four to five inches) but thin, triangular or leaf-shaped tools which have been bifacially retouched. In western Europe, such tools are rare except for a span of a few thousand years (between 18,000 and 20,000 years ago) when bifacially flaked leaf-shaped tools are found in sites west of the Rhône and in Spain in layers referred to as Solutrean.

The French Solutrean has left us the most spectacular examples of Paleolithic stone chipping, notably the almost unbelievably delicate and handsome Solutrean *laurel leaves* (see *Figure* 34). The largest laurel leaf ever found was part of a cache of seventeen blades stacked together found near Volgu, sixty miles north-east of Lyon in eastern France. This magnificent blade, unfortunately broken, was originally about 13¾ inches long, ¾ inches at its widest, and only slightly more than ¼ of an inch thick.

These knappers knew how to remove very regular flakes to shape their tools. Some of these flakes were more than two inches in length and had a very small bulb and attenuated ripples leaving very flat scars on the face of the tools being worked. Many Solutrean flakes show a carefully prepared chipped platform at the butt, demonstrating the use of the technique known as the "turned edge" discussed previously in the description of the manufacture of fine Acheulian bifaces. It is probable that the larger laurel leaves were also made by soft-hammer percussion, in view of their characteristics.

It is reasonable to assume that the smaller, thicker laurel leaves were hafted to wooden shafts and used as projectile points. However, this seems to have been an unlikely use for the larger ones. The obvious fragility of some of the specimens suggest rather a ritual use, or perhaps they were simply examples of some knapper's bravura. Quite possibly the laurel leaves were also used as knives, probably simply held in a piece of leather in the hand.

The striking fineness and regularity in the parallelism of the long and narrow flake scars on the surface peculiar to the Solutrean tools—notably the smaller ones such as the small laurel leaves, the unifacially flaked willow leaves and the shouldered

Figure 32. Multiple tool: dihedral burin at top end and end-scraper below.

Figure 33. Multiple tool: Scraper at top end, burin on oblique truncation below.

Figure 34. Height of craftsmanship among Paleolithic workers in flint is the Solutrean "laurel leaf" blade. This specimen from Volgu measures over a foot long, a quarter-inch thick.

points (see *Figures* 35, 36, 37) have suggested to archaeologists that other flaking techniques which afforded greater control than direct percussion might have been used by the Solutrean knappers. Indirect percussion using a punch applied on the prepared-edge platform is a possibility, for instance. However, there is good evidence that "pressure flaking" was used to some extent. This technique, probably known in earlier times but apparently rarely used, allows far greater precision in chipping stone, but the flakes removed are smaller than those with percussion flaking (*Figure* 22–7, 8). The implements used for pressure flaking might sometimes have been nothing more than a stone flake with a square edge, or the surface of an anvil stone. More usually, it was probably an implement of hard wood, antler, or bone (*Figure* 38) called a *retouchoir,* some of which have been found as early as the Mousterian period. One end or one side of the retouchoir was applied close to the edge of the tool to be worked, preferably on a prepared platform, and then pressed strongly with a forward thrust, detaching a flake (*Figure* 39). These flakes have a very flat bulb and practically no ripples and leave therefore very fine and flat scars on the blank being worked. A helpful analogy explaining these features might be to compare the strong waves produced by throwing an object into a pool of water, as opposed to the small ripples produced when the same object is slowly immersed.

Stone materials vary in their response to pressure flaking. Volcanic rocks seem particularly well suited to this technique. There are descriptions dating from the sixteenth century of Mexican knappers flaking long, narrow, obsidian blades with extraordinary regularity by using large pressure implements to which handles and crossbars had been affixed to enable the knapper to add the strength of his shoulder or chest. Mr. Donald Crabtree, an extremely gifted knapper from Idaho who collaborates with archaeologists, was consistently able to obtain fine obsidian blades more than eight inches in length by imitating the Mexican techniques. Flint, however, is a coarser and tougher material. It appears on the basis of experiments and of the ethnological observations of Australian aborigines, who are masters of this technique, that the maximum length of the flake removed by pressure is generally under three quarters of an inch in length.

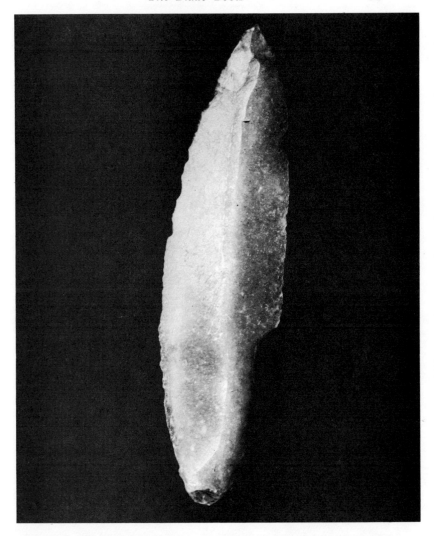

Figure 35. This shouldered point and those in *Figures* 36 and 37 illustrate some variations of Solutrean flaking technique. Each point has been made by retouching blades. The two-inch point, *above,* made from a small, narrow blade, has had only part of the edge retouched, to assist hafting. The stem of the point in *Figure* 36 is more extensively worked on one face, and the third point (*Figure* 37) has been pressure-flaked over the entire surface.

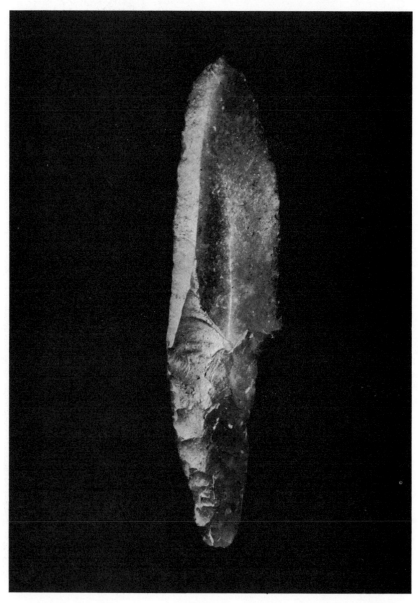

Figure 36. The haft end of this three-inch point has been pressure-flaked on one face only.

Figure 37. Two-inch point pressure-flaked over both faces.

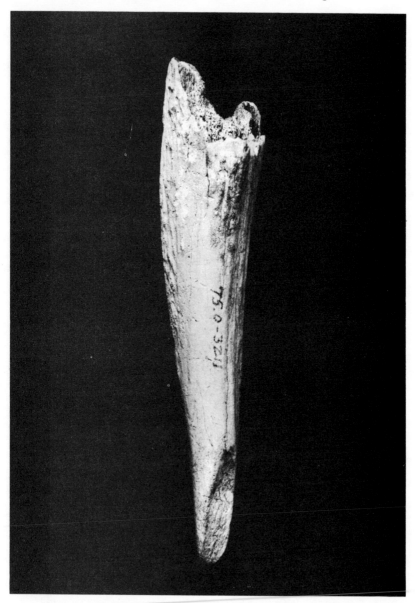

Figure 38. Fragment of bone or antler served as pressure flaker; this antler flaker, or retouchoir, dates from the Mesolithic.

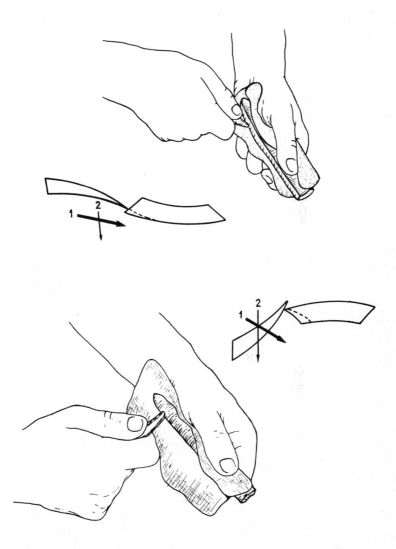

Figure 39. The art of retouching reached its height within the Upper Paleolithic with the technique of pressure flaking shown here in drawings. The flaking tool, perhaps a length of antler, was applied directly to the blade's edge. A forward and a downward thrust (note the component arrows) detached a flake.

It was therefore of great interest to learn of Mr. Crabtree's recent experiments with flint which definitely show that it can be made to yield larger flakes, after having been heated. There are some indications in the ethnological literature that knappers heat flint before flaking it by percussion, but it was Mr. Crabtree who demonstrated first that flint heated to a relatively high temperature yields, with the pressure technique, flakes up to two inches in length, i.e. three to four times the length obtained with unheated flint. Professor Bordes, who has collaborated with Mr. Crabtree, has since pointed out that some of the Solutrean tools have the lustrous surface and the slightly greasy feel characteristic of heated flint, suggesting that this technique was known in the Upper Paleolithic.

During the Magdalenian, the period that followed the Solutrean in France and lasted until the end of glacial times, the manufacture of the elegant stone leaves was abandoned. Magdalenian settlements in caves and open sites are large and numerous, indicating, in some cases, permanent occupation. Their economy was based mainly on hunting reindeer herds and fishing salmon. For us, Magdalenians are remarkable for the striking beauty of their polychrome mural paintings (such as those found at Altamira in Spain) and for their bone and antler implements—harpoons and spear heads, spear throwers, and other implements, often beautifully carved and sculptured.

Except for a few new tools (see *Figure* 22–10, 11, 26) the Magdalenian tool kit contained tools common to all the Upper Paleolithic industries, though, as usual, types vary in predominance according to the time and region. It is notable, however, that there was an increasing use of bladelets and of very small blade fragments, retouched into geometric shapes, often less than one inch long, called "microliths." These microliths, hafted into grooved shafts or handles, mark the eventual culmination of the trend toward smaller flint implements. They became even more important in a later period, the Mesolithic, in immediately post-glacial times.

In eastern and central Europe, Upper Paleolithic man shared many tools with man of western Europe. However, there are differences, especially in the composition of tool kits in the various areas. Worked ivory, relatively rare in the west, is common from sites of eastern and central Europe, where mammoth was the main quarry. Numerous huts and shelters dug part way into the ground, a form of dwelling apparently not used in western Europe, are often found outlined with rows of mammoth bones and tusks.

Elsewhere in the Old World, much less is known about the technology of the groups of man contemporary with the European blade-tool users. The Middle Eastern stone tools are relatively close to the European types. But in the rest of Asia the Chopper and Chopping tool tradition, and in Africa south of the Sahara, the Levallois and Mousterian tools lasted for a long period, and were replaced only very much later—in some areas only in the post-glacial—by blade and bladelet industries resembling the European Upper Paleolithic tool complexes.

Prehistoric life in Europe at the end of the Upper Paleolithic exemplifies a remarkably successful exploitation of the environment by hunting, fishing, and gathering. The specialized and diversified implements of stone, bone, and antler, the large and numerous settlements, sometimes permanent, the huge accumulations of bones of hunted animals (mammoth, reindeer and horse), the cave art in southwestern Europe, female figurines, decorated bone and antler implements, and the personal ornaments found with burials, all give an impression of life in the Upper Paleolithic which is quite different from the drab and hectic life of men on the verge of starvation that has so often been pictured as the life of our Paleolithic ancestors. Archaeological and ethnological studies suggest a quite different picture.

Intensive studies of the subsistence and work patterns of primitive bands of modern hunters and gatherers such as the Bushmen of the Kalahari Desert in South Africa, or the Australian aborigines have shown that sufficient amounts of food can be obtained with surprisingly little effort, even from such marginal environments, to feed these small bands of men.

As long as there are no drastic changes in the environment, subsistence crises would normally occur for hunters and gatherers only when the number of people living in a particular area approaches too closely the maximum number that can be fed through the use of a particular technology. Given the natural growth of populations, and barring any demographic upsets such as epidemic diseases, there are essentially three factors that serve to keep populations below the critical number. These are: wars or feuds, migrations, and birth control. Archaeologists have been unable to find much evidence for conflict in Paleolithic times. But the fact that man migrated into unoccupied territories is quite evident. By the end of the Upper Paleolithic all habitable territories were known to man, including Australia and the New World, and were occupied with varying density. As for population control, there is clear ethnological evidence that hunters and gatherers practiced birth control in the form of sex taboos, contraception, abortion, and infanticide. The number of infants that can be brought along during the nomadic subsistence cycle is obviously limited, and it is quite likely that Paleolithic man must also have resorted to birth control of some form during this period.

During the Upper Paleolithic, the hunting of large herds of animals brought a certain measure of sedentism and probably made possible an increase in the size of the family unit, and consequently of the population within the settlements. Upper Paleolithic man lived in a variety of environments that were much richer than those of present-day hunters and gatherers, and he probably reached a higher level of prosperity and attained a degree of cultural elaboration about which, unfortunately, very little will ever be known.

The span of the Magdalenian culture—the last and most impressive of the Paleolithic cultures—lasted five or six thousand years. About 10,000 years ago, the glaciers started to melt, raising the level of the sea. Lands, freed from the huge masses of ice that covered them, slowly lifted up. Changes in the flora and fauna took place, especially near the ice sheets of the northern hemisphere. As the vegetation belts moved northward, new ways of life, new implements, and new ways of working stone were developed to deal with the new conditions. It was in these early post-glacial times, referred to by archaeologists as the Mesolithic, that these developments took place.

VI
Microliths and Ground Stone Tools

In certain regions of the Old World, especially those close to the glaciated regions, the Mesolithic was for prehistoric man a period of drastic adjustment to the new environment. It eventually terminated with the adoption of cultivation and animal husbandry. These skills progressively complemented and then replaced hunting, fishing, and gathering to different degrees in various areas.

We will now direct our attention mainly to the developments in stone tool technology that took place in Southwest Asia and Europe. There are two reasons for this. The first is that these are the best-known areas archaeologically, since extensive work has been going on there for a long time. The second is that the quality of the stonework in these areas is superior, especially in southern Scandinavia, where the retreating glaciers had uncovered large outcrops of flint of the best possible quality. As research progresses in other areas, the picture will become more complete. For there is evidence that the Near Eastern European "neolithic" cultural development was not unique, and that other original centers of domestication of plants and animals and technological innovations existed in eastern or southeastern Asia and in West Africa.

In Europe, with the end of the Pleistocene, the tundras and steppes with their vast herds of animals were replaced by almost boundless expanses of coniferous and deciduous forests. In dense forests, game is neither so plentiful nor so easily tracked as on the open plains. The remains of Mesolithic cultures generally reflect this impoverishment: they were much less spec-

Figure 40. Miniature size of some Mesolithic implements shown by comparison with the point of a Neolithic dagger, *center*. The inch-long nucleus, *left*, furnished tiny blades; larger blade fragments, *right*, were retouched in geometric shapes.

Figure 41. Microliths were used in a variety of ways, by setting the sharp flints in wood, bone, or antler. This bone point is six inches in length; its "barbs" are fixed with resin cement.

tacular than those left by the Upper Paleolithic hunters of horse, reindeer, and mammoth. Mesolithic man left us no cave paintings and very little carving on bone or antler. Nonetheless, he was most resourceful in adapting to the new conditions, and he soon occupied the new areas freed by the ice. New implements and new ways of working stone were invented. In southwestern Asia, the first experimentations were made on the new modes of subsistence, modes that were to have tremendous cultural consequences, the domestication of plants and animals.

In Europe, where the most important environmental changes took place, a great deal of information has come from the Maglemosian sites of northwestern Europe which are often found in peat bogs and are therefore relatively well preserved. This culture, which spread from England to Russia between 6000 and 8000 B.C., complemented hunting, as did most other Mesolithic cultures, with an intensive exploitation of other sources of food. Evidence of fowling, and the gathering of nuts and generally of all wild plant food becomes extensive. The recovery of bone fish spear heads (single or multipronged), barbless bone fish hooks, traps, and nets (with weights and floats) indicates that Mesolithic man was systematically collecting other sources of protein than the wild game of the forests. In late Mesolithic times in northwestern Europe (i.e. approximately in the fourth or fifth millennium), some coastal groups left huge accumulations of mollusk shells, and of the bones of sea mammals and ocean fishes.

There were also important changes in hunting methods. Tracking and bringing down game in the forests was made easier by man's use of dogs. The bow and arrow, probably invented in the late Upper Paleolithic, became the principal weapon. More accurate than spear throwers and spears, especially for smaller game, the bow and arrow is also more practical to use for forest hunting.

The most characteristic flint implements of the Mesolithic are the microliths, the very small flints that first appeared in the Magdalenian and sometimes even earlier levels of the Upper Paleolithic (*Figure* 40). Varying in size from a half-inch to two inches, they were designed to form the points or the cutting and carving edges of a number of wooden or bone implements. Arrows, for example, usually were tipped or barbed with these small flints (*Figure* 41).

Microliths were manufactured from very small blade nuclei sometimes no more than an inch high and were worked with a punch and hammer, or perhaps rather by pressure. A later method consisted of fragmenting larger blades by means of a notching technique sometimes called the micro-burin technique. Once flaked or fragmented, the tiny flints were frequently retouched until they assumed standardized geometric forms such as crescents, triangles, and trapezes (*Figure* 42).

The microliths represent the final stage of the technological evolution in the reduction in the size of chipped stone implements. According to Professor Leroi-Gourhan, more than 300 feet of cutting edge can, theoretically, be obtained from two pounds of flint by using it to manufacture microliths. In making microliths, flint is thriftily restricted to a replaceable working edge which is held in a bone or antler haft. Conceptually, it can be compared to the modern tools where only the cutting edges are made out of the best materials and the edge or point can be changed when worn without having to replace the whole tool.

The manufacture of microliths began before the end of the Pleistocene, but became more prevalent in post-glacial times in the Old World. South Africa was probably the last area to adopt the new technique, around 1000 B.C.

Apparently rare in southern China and southeastern Asia, geometric microliths were found in Australia dating back to 3000 B.C. They are quite common in southern India where their first appearance, while difficult to date, may probably go back to 4000 B.C. Microliths were also quite common in Siberia and are probably much older there since a date of 12,000 years ago has recently been obtained for Japanese microliths.

In Europe, it was also in post-glacial times that Mesolithic man started to develop new types of heavy stone tools for felling and shaping timber.

The first evidence for flaked axes and adzes with ground edges dates from about the ninth millennium in northwestern Europe and southwestern Asia, but surprisingly early dates of about 20,000 years ago have recently been obtained for axes with ground edges found in Japan and in northern Australia.

The dampness of the northwestern Mesolithic peat bogs has

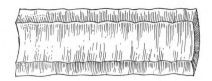

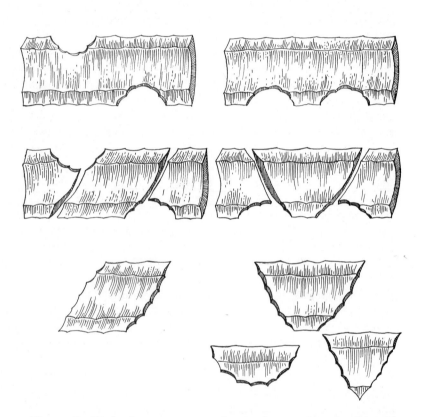

Figure 42. Blade fragments were also used to make microliths. If notched on opposite sides, *left,* the blade—when broken—yielded a chip that could be flaked into rhomboidal form. When notched on the same side, *right,* the broken blade provided a central fragment that could be retouched into a variety of shapes: a trapeze, lunate, or a triangular form, *bottom right.* (The small ends of the notched blades have been often called *microburins* because of their resemblance to burins on truncation. However, there is little evidence that they were used as such, and they were probably thrown off as waste.)

preserved a number of celts (i.e. ax and adz blades) inserted into antler sleeves which were themselves perforated for the insertion of wooden handles. The technique used to obtain many of these early celts is called the *tranchet* technique. It resembles the method used in manufacturing the old Lower Paleolithic cleavers, since the bit of the bifacially flaked celts is the original edge of a thick flake. Soon, however, around 7000 B.C., a number of celts began to have ground edges, and sometimes the entire celt was shaped by grinding. It was with these new types of woodworking tools that Mesolithic man manufactured the many new implements that have been pre-served in the northwestern European sites: dugout canoes, staves for skin-covered boats, paddles, and eventually sledges and skis and other implements that served these populations to spread into new areas and aided in their exploitation of the food to be found in lakes, rivers, and seas.

The importance of this new stone technology was to increase considerably with the introduction of food-producing techniques into Europe. In the Mesolithic, the felling and shaping of timber had been largely limited to the wood required to make hunting and fishing equipment and to build relatively simple dwellings. The European forest cover remained almost unchanged until the sixth millennium B.C., when a "Neolithic" complex of Near Eastern origin began to spread into southeastern Europe: villages of agglomerated mud brick or mud walls and timbered houses; cultivation of wheat and barley; the breeding of sheep, goats, swine, and cattle; and ceramics and weaving. These forest-clearing farmers started their great spread from this area toward central and northwestern Europe during the fifth millennium. By 4500 B.C. the European plains from the Rhine to the Dniester were occupied by a culturally uniform population of farmers whom archaeologists call Danubians or Linear Pottery People.

The earlier hunting and fishing people of Europe had settled mainly near lakes, rivers, and seas. Only rarely did they populate densely forested areas. But for these immigrant farmers, dense forest vegetation meant fertile soil, land which was, furthermore, easier to clear than the tough sod of the open plains which was eventually to yield only to plow agriculture. The evidence points to a type of cultivation—called slash and burn or swidden

—involving the repeated clearing of patches of forest by felling the trees or simply ringing them with axes to kill their foliage, and then burning the sparse underbrush. Then after a few harvests, the superficial layer of the soil became exhausted and the farmers moved on to new ground. The communities of these early cultivators grew rapidly. A typical community probably numbered between two hundred and six hundred members. When its population increased beyond this maximum, a new group would branch off and clear a new area of its own. Never staying in the same location more than a few years, during which they enjoyed the initial richness of the newly cleared soil, these groups diffused rapidly over most of Europe, deforesting much of the land.

The shifting type of cultivation practiced by these early settlers did not prevent them from building villages of substantial wooden houses, which were sometimes reinhabited when the soil had lain fallow long enough to regain fertility. Examples of such early Neolithic houses, excavated at Köln-Lindenthal, in northwestern Germany, were built of timber and measured thirty to a hundred feet long by fifteen to twenty feet in width. These structures, with mud-plastered walls, probably were used as both granaries and living quarters. This village seems to have been rebuilt perhaps seven times, and included about twenty houses each sheltering some twenty people, members of several families. It has been estimated that each occupation of the village lasted about ten years, followed by a fifty-year abandonment, during which the land that had been under cultivation would have regained its fertility.

Both the great importance of forest clearance in this new economy and the extensive use of timber in building made the adz, ax, and such other carpentry tools as chisels, gouges, and wedges a most important part of the equipment of these farmers (see *Figures* 43 through 46). It will be recalled that some Mesolithic celts, although shaped by flaking, had their working edges ground by abrasion. This technique of shaping stone tools became predominant among the agriculturalists. They usually employed grinding to shape the entire implement. It was for this reason that the early prehistorians called the new era the age of New (i.e. grinding method) Stone, or Neolithic, in con-

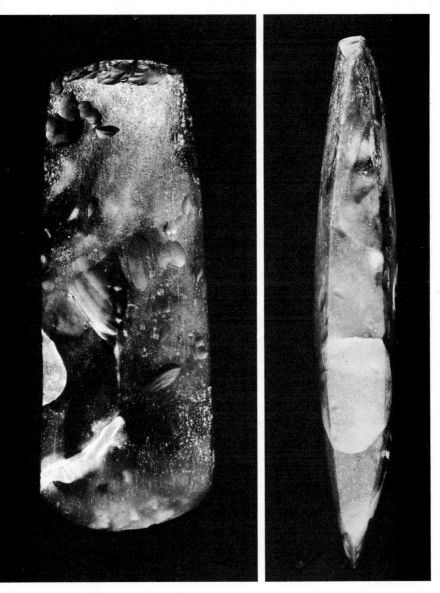

Figure 43. Axhead, from a Danish Neolithic site, is seen in front, *above,* and side view, *opposite, Figure* 44. Six inches long, the tool was brought to final form by grinding and polishing.

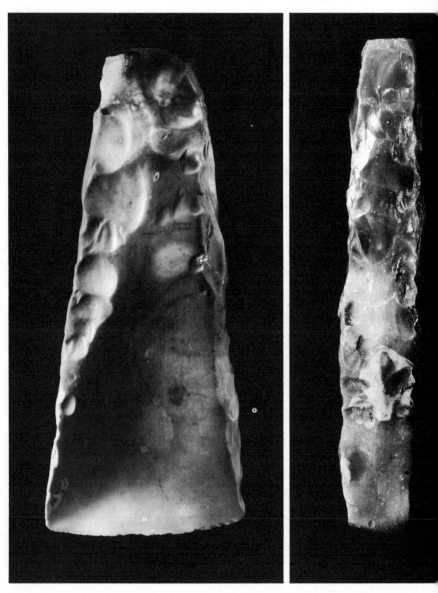

Figure 45. Carpentry tools, from the Danish Neolithic, are, *above,* a hollow-ground gouge and, *opposite,* a chisel, *Figure* 46. The grinding is limited to working edges.

trast to the age of Old (i.e. flaking method) Stone, or Paleolithic.

The advantage of a polished celt (polishing refers particularly to the last and finest grinding) has been demonstrated experimentally. Wood can be chopped faster with this type of tool. The smooth head penetrates deeper than a flaked ax, and the strong, symmetrical edge withstands the force of the blow much better than a flaked edge, which, because of unequal distribution of stresses, is more likely to break or chip. Indeed, polished axes are remarkably durable and efficient. Modern experimenters felled a fir tree more than two feet in diameter in eighteen minutes with such an ax, while oaks more than a foot in diameter were cut down in half an hour without any damage to the polished stone blade.

To manufacture a polished stone celt, a nodule was first flaked into a shape approximating that of the desired implement (*Figure* 47). This rough blank was then ground by rubbing on slabs or outcroppings of gritty rock, such as sandstone. The finish, or final polish, was usually obtained by rubbing the implement with a finer-grained stone, using sand as an abrasive. Wetting the sand gave a smoother finish. Portable grinders, presumably used to resharpen the celt's edges when necessary, have been found.

The over-all efficiency of an ax or adz depends in large measure on the way it is mounted on a handle. Most Neolithic celt handles were cut from the roots or branches of oak or ash.

Generally, the stone tool was then mounted in one or two fashions: either the celt was perforated, permitting the introduction of a handle, or the handle was perforated or mortised, so that the celt could be set into the wooden handle.

The first would seem to be the better method: perforated tool heads are usual with the axes and hammers of today, while some mace heads were mounted in this fashion as long ago as the Mesolithic in northern Europe. However, this method of mounting was rarely used during the Neolithic. One probable reason lies in the effort required to drill through stone without the help of metal tools. Indeed, consider the steps involved in the earliest method. First, sink a lead hole in the tool's side by means of percussion with a hammerstone. Then, with a round wooden stick and sand, bore the hole deeper. Because most of

Figure 47. Flint "blanks," like this Danish one, were common trade items during the Neolithic. They were roughed into shape by percussion at quarries where superior flint was available and traded in this unfinished form. Then they were worked into finished adz or ax blades by the process of grinding.

the abrasion is done by the sides of the revolving stick, and very little by the tip, it is necessary, after a time, to use percussion on the tool again, pounding a new lead in the bottom of the cavity, then, back to drilling. However, after a certain depth is reached, it becomes impossible to use the hammerstone to sink a new lead in the bottom of the cavity without widening the entire hole excessively. The implement is therefore turned over and the same procedure repeated until the two holes meet at the center. Even so, the shape of the resulting biconical perforation resembles an hourglass.

A great improvement over this laborious method was the hollow-boring method. A bone or hollow reed is rotated as a drill, with sand for an abrasive. This cuts a cylindrical core, which falls out when the opposite side of the tool is reached. Thus, a perfect perforation is obtained, with far less work involved than in the earlier, biconical technique. Use of bow drills presumably further reduced the investment in time.

Despite such improved techniques, few perforated stone implements have been recovered from the Neolithic. For, quite aside from the work involved, the shaft hole through the stone weakened the implement excessively. The shock of each blow, combined with the strain caused by wedging of the handle, tended to break the celt in a short time. Hence, the Neolithic preference for the second method of hafting-perforating or mortising the handle itself. One means of doing this was to place the celt directly into a perforation or a mortise in the handle (see *Figure* 48).

The disadvantage of this method was that the shocks of use drove the celt into the softer, wooden handle, and eventually split it. But, another means of mounting already known from Mesolithic of northwestern Europe could be used to prevent the handle from splitting. It consisted of using an antler socket as an intermediate piece. This socket acted as a shock absorber, while a stop ridge, ground around the socket (or sometimes a thick spur), prevented the celt from being driven through the handle by use (see *Figures* 49 and 50, *top*).

Another particularly efficient means of mounting, especially for adzes, was knee-shaft hafting. For this type of hafting, a short section of a sturdy sapling with a projecting branch was selected. The trunk portion was then split to accommodate the celt, while the branch served as a handle. In other cases, the celt was lashed to the side of the trunk portion (*Figure 50, bottom*). While the latter would not seem to be as strong as a split mounting, it has the advantage of allowing the adz blade to strike almost parallel to the surface of the wood being dressed.

Knee-shaft hafting was very popular, and not only in Neolithic times. In later periods, knee-shaft hafting was used for metal tools in most of northern Europe. Its main advantages lay in simplicity of manufacture, good balance and the fact that the blade did not tend to split the handle (as did the blade set in a perforated handle).

Increasing demands for stone of good quality for heavy wood-working tools during this period must have depleted a great number of Europe's most accessible sources of flint. Neolithic man began to mine extensively for this material. Shafts as deep as fifty feet, sometimes connected by radial galleries about six

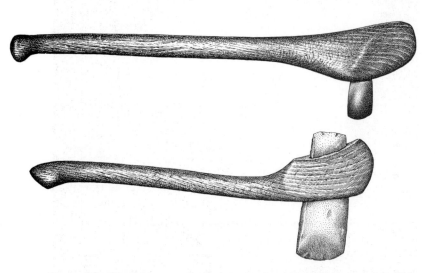

Figure 48. Neolithic axes hafted in perforated or mortised handles. The three-and-a-half-inch celt, *top,* was set in mortise in a wooden handle. The seven-and-a-half-inch celt, *bottom,* was set in a perforated handle.

Figure 49. Antler socket with its base cut to fit a wooden handle served as a shock absorber for this Neolithic celt.

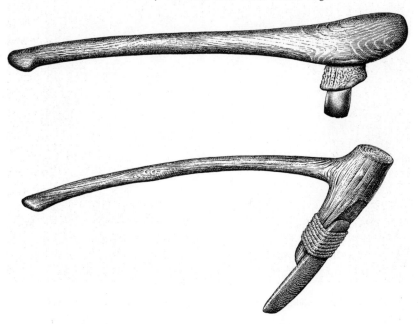

Figure 50. Ax and adz of the Neolithic. Adz blades are asymmetrically beveled and set at right angles to the handle. The improved hafting technique, *top,* sets ax blade in antler shock absorber to help prevent the splitting of the handle. Adz hafted at an angle, *bottom,* was used for dressing wood. Its haft is made out of a sapling limb and trunk.

feet high, have been found at Spiennes in Belgium. At Grimes Graves, in Norfolk, the mined area covers more than thirty-four acres. Flint of superior flaking quality was mined there, as well as at locations in northern and northwestern Europe and there is reason to believe that the mining was done by local specialists, who preflaked the nodules into rough shapes and traded them in this "blank" form.

The shortage in supplies of flint of good quality, and of other flakable stone, was alleviated by the extensive use of a third technique of stone-shaping, one which made possible the manufacture of tools from many sorts of common stone. The new development employed a crumbling, battering or pecking method. Earlier man had already used this technique to a limited extent.

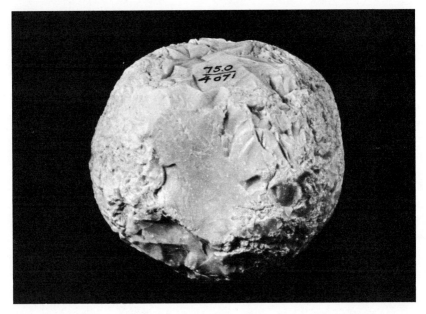

Figure 51. Flint pecking stone measuring three inches in diameter.

In southwestern Asia, querns, mortars and pestles, bowls, and ornaments made of ground stone are found at several sites dating to the ninth millennium B.C. Examples of stone celts, made partially or entirely by grinding were made not much later in southwestern Asia and then in northwestern Europe, but it is only with the spread of farming that the shaping of stone implements by crumbling found wide use. In combination with grinding, this technique permitted a great number of dense, fine-grained stones of high tenacity to be used for implements, material that could not have been satisfactorily shaped by flaking.

This process consisted of "hammer-dressing" the potential tool's surface; by crumbling it away with repeated light blows of different sized hammerstones until the "blank" attained the required shape. Hammerstones of flint were especially useful for this repeated pecking. Not only was flint's superior hardness an asset, but the repeated blows against the tool detached minute flakes from the flint hammerstone, leaving hundreds of very sharp edges, which acted like so many tiny chisels on the surface of the stone being shaped (see *Figure* 51). Once pecked to rough shape, the implement was finished by grinding. Still another way to shape implements of non-flakable stone was by sawing, using retouched flint blades or sand as the cutting agent, and wood or bone as the "saw."

These new methods—pecking and grinding tools out of common stone—were, of course, much more time-consuming than the flaking techniques. Contemporary studies of Australian aborigines have allowed us to break down the time required to manufacture a stone ax. For example, a diorite ax about eight inches long, four inches wide and two inches in thickness can, with luck, be roughed out by flaking in a few minutes. Pecking the surface of the ax, to remove the flake scars, takes an additional day or two, and grinding and polishing the ax to final finish, with sand and water on a slab of sandstone, consumes a further two days. The length of time varies, of course, with the fineness of the stone's grain and the size of the implement desired. It is noteworthy that contemporary Australian quarries like the prehistoric European ones are littered with unfinished implements, rejected because of a break due to an ill-placed blow or a flaw in the stone.

The northward and westward spread of the farming cultures has already been traced to some extent by archaeologists. By 2500 B.C., the ax- and adz-using peasants had occupied most of Europe. There is no doubt, however, that hunting, fishing, and gathering cultures, some of which adopted a few of the farmer's cultural innovations, persisted for a long time in many regions which were not particularly favorable for cultivation. And in some cases, vast regions, such as northeastern Europe, remained exclusively the domain of the heirs to the Mesolithic ways of life until the first millennium B.C.

The excavation of the farming villages indicates a prosperous and peaceful life. But in later times—possibly because the fast-growing population competed for the better agricultural and pasture lands—one finds these villages protected by moats and palisades, while stone weapons appear in large numbers.

One look at the stone axes illustrated in *Figure* 52 will suffice to indicate that their conception is totally different from that of the stone implements previously manufactured. For these are careful copies in stone of metal originals, the extremely rare

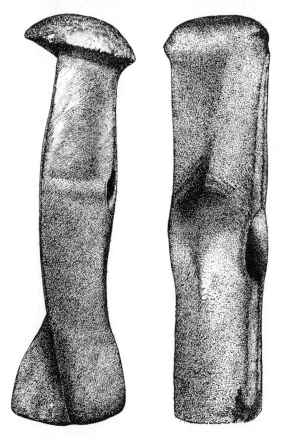

Figure 52. Danish Neolithic weapons are meticulous copies, in ground stone, of originals made out of copper. In this drawing the battle-ax on the left is seven inches long; the weapon on the right shows the casting seams of the metal prototype.

and precious copper axes that were so admired and envied by the late Neolithic farmers of northern Europe around 2500 B.C. The splayed edge of one specimen is reminiscent of the splaying of a repeatedly hammered copper blade; the longitudinal ridge simulates the seam of a metal piece that has been cast in a closed mold. And, in both, the shaft holes are features more suited to metal than to stone, for we have seen that celts are excessively weakened by such holes.

The metal originals that inspired these battle-axes and the flint daggers (see *Figures* 53 and 54) were probably manu-factured in one of the early centers of metalworking which had been established by Aegean or Anatolian smiths in Romania, Hungary, and Slovakia, or in Portugal and Spain, near the newly discovered European copper-ore deposits.

Early copper and bronze implements were no sharper than flint implements, but they had a number of other important advantages besides their prestige value. First, metal is not so brittle as stone: where a celt may break or chip, copper or bronze merely bends. Axes, adzes, and saws of metal are more efficient than stone for cutting wood, because they can be made thinner and thus cut deeper. Moreover, by casting, metal can be formed in a wide variety of shapes and worn-out tools may be remelted and cast anew.

In spite of all these advantages, stone was only slowly re-placed by metal. At first, use of copper and bronze was re-stricted to ornaments and weapons. Only later were these metals used for craft tools, such as the ax, the adz, and the saw, and the use of metal for domestic and agricultural implements came much later and was not common. Indeed, it was not until the last centuries before Christ, when iron, a more abundant metal, was introduced, that the tradition of stone implements was largely abandoned in Europe. In certain regions such as the Mediter-ranean, flint blades continued to be used to line the undersides of the heavy wooden sledges which were pulled by oxen over the threshing floors to separate the grains from the stalks and chop up the straw. This ancient technique is still very common in Turkey today.

In other parts of the world, implements of chipped and ground stone continued to be used. In the New World, stone implements, some as magnificent as the Danish daggers of the Old World, were knapped. Indeed, these New World stone tools and weapons brought about De Jussieu's suggestion, in 1723, that the ceraunias were actually the implements of early in-habitants of Europe. At about the same time, the flintlock fire-arm was invented, and for about a century, until the invention

Figure 53. The ultimate skill in the art of stone flaking is displayed by this Late Danish Neolithic copy of a metal dagger. The weapon is over ten inches long but only a quarter of an inch thick. The first step was to grind the flint blank to a symmetrical shape after which the surface was flaked from prepared platforms.

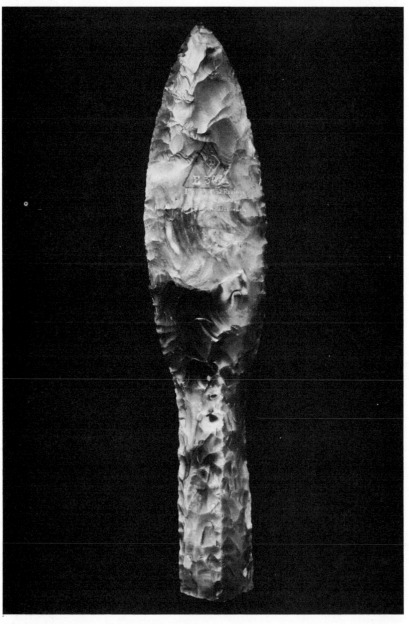

Figure 54. Late Danish Neolithic copy of a metal dagger with its handle. The weapon is eight inches long.

of the percussion cap, this new use for flint gave rise to an important industry. At Meusne in France and at Brandon in England, both sources of good flint, millions of gunflints were produced during this period. Shortly after the invention of the percussion cap, in the 1830s, friction matches were invented, and the ancient method of making fire with tinder and the sparks of flint struck by iron pyrites or steel was slowly abandoned.

Today the two-million-year-old art of manufacturing tools and weapons from stone is, in the main, known only to scholars concerned with prehistory. Pecking and grinding techniques, in turn, are still used by sculptors, masons, and lapidarists. In a few areas of the world, all these ancient techniques—percussion flaking, pressure flaking, pecking, and grinding—are still used by a handful of hunting and gathering peoples. These peoples are the last to use stone for tools and weapons—the last heirs to a technological tradition that made it possible for early man to survive, spread over the earth, and to establish the base of mankind's cultural development.

Key to Bibliography*

HISTORY OF RESEARCH

Bibby, 1956; Cartailhac, 1877; Childe, 1941; *Daniel, 1950, 1964, 1967;* Déchelette, 1908; Evans, 1897; Jussieu, 1725; Laming-Emperaire, 1964; Lubbock, 1913; Mortillet and Mortillet, 1900; Movius, 1949b; Peyrony, 1948; Sollas, 1924; Sonneville-Bordes, 1967; Vayson de Pradenne, 1932.

METHODS

Binford and Binford, 1966, 1969; Bohmers, 1963; Bordes, 1950, 1961b, 1967; Brézillon, 1968; Brothwell and Higgs, 1963; *Clark, J. G. D.,* 1952, *1957;* Crabtree, 1966; Crabtree and Davis, 1968; Garrod, 1946; Goodwin, 1953; Heinzelin de Braucourt, 1962; Heizer and Cook, 1960; *Hole and Heizer, 1969; Laming-Emperaire, 1963;* Laplace-Jauretche, 1957; Laplace, 1966; Laplace, 1968; Lee and Devore, 1968; Leroi-Gourhan, 1943, 1945, 1964b, 1965a; Leroi-Gourhan and others, 1966; Movius, 1949b; Oakley, 1954; Sackett, 1966; Semenov, 1964; Sonnenfeld, 1962; Sonneville-Bordes and Perrot, 1953; Squier, 1953; Swanson, 1966; Tixier, 1963; Wilmsen, 1968a, 1968b.

GEOCHRONOLOGY AND ENVIRONMENT

Brothwell and Higgs, 1963; *Butzer,* 1964, *1965;* Charlesworth, 1957; Clarke, J. D., 1960; Flint, 1957; Harlan and Zohari, 1966; Howell and Bourlière, 1963; Lavocat and others, 1966; Lee and Devore, 1968; McBurney, 1950; Zeuner, 1958, 1959.

MANUALS AND SUMMARIES

OLD WORLD, GENERAL

Barnett, 1961; *Bordes,* 1967, *1968; Braidwood, 1967;* Brézillon, 1968; Clark, J. D., 1963, 1966; Clark, J. D. and Howell, 1966; *Clark, J. G. D.,* 1961, *1967; Clark, J. G. D. and Piggott, 1965;* Coon, 1962b; Déchelette, 1908; Ehrich, 1965; *Howell, 1965;* Howells, 1967; *Leroi-Gourhan and others, 1966;* Mortillet and

* Recommended introductory authors are in italic.

Mortillet, 1900; Movius, 1949b, 1956; *Oakley*, 1957a, *1964;* Sankalia, 1964; Singer, Holmyard, and Hall, 1954; *Sonneville-Bordes*, 1961, *1967*.

PALEOLITHIC, EUROPE AND SOUTHWEST ASIA

Alimen, 1965; Bordaz, 1959a; Bordes, 1950, 1961a; Braidwood and Howe, 1957; Breuil, 1913; Breuil and Lantier, 1959; Evans, 1897; Garrod and Clark, J. G. D., 1965; Howell, 1966; Klindt-Jensen, 1957; Leroi-Gourhan, 1949, 1955; McBurney, 1950; Noone, 1949; Peyrony, 1948; Pradel, 1958; Smith, P. E. L., 1964, 1966a; Société Préhistorique Française, 1954; Sonneville-Bordes, 1960; Taute, 1965; Valoch, 1968.

MESOLITHIC AND NEOLITHIC EUROPE AND SOUTHWEST ASIA

Bailloud and Mieg de Boofzheim, 1955; Becker, 1945, 1959; Bibby, 1956; Binford, L. R., 1968; Bohmers, 1963; Bordaz, 1959b; Braidwood and Howe, 1957; Cann and Renfrew, 1964; Childe, 1941, 1956; Clark, J. G. D., 1936, 1945, 1947, 1952, 1954, 1962, 1965; Darby, 1956; Dixon, Cann and Renfrew, 1968; Dyson, 1964; Garrod and J. G. D. Clark, 1965; Evans, 1897; Flannery, 1965; Gabel, 1958a, 1958b; Grantzau, 1954; Harlan and Zohari, 1966; Houlder, 1961; Howell, 1959; Klindt-Jensen, 1957; Mellaart, 1965; Piggott, 1965; Renfrew, Dixon and Cann, 1966; Strahm, 1961, 1962; Taute, 1965; Waterbolk, 1968; Zeuner, 1964.

ASIA AND AUSTRALIA

Allchin, 1957; Chang, 1963a, 1963b, 1968; Ikawa, 1968; McCarthy, 1943; McCarthy, Bramell and Noone, 1946; Movius, 1944, 1949a, 1949c; Mulvaney, 1961, 1965; Sankalia, 1963, 1967; Walker and Sieveking, 1962; White, 1967.

AFRICA

Alimen, 1955; Balout, 1955; Bishop and J. D. Clark, 1963; Clark, J. D., 1958, 1959, 1960, 1967; Cole, 1963; Goodwin, 1953; Howell and Bourlière, 1963; Howell and Clark, 1963; Leakey, L. S. B., 1951; Leakey, M. D., 1963; McBurney, 1960; Mason, 1962; Ramendo, 1963; Tixier, 1963.

PHYSICAL ANTHROPOLOGY

Brace, 1967; *Brace and Montagu, 1965; Clark, W. LeGros, 1964,* 1967; *Coon, 1962a,* 1962b; Day, 1965; Everden and Curtis and others, 1965; Howell, 1964; *Howells, 1967;* Jullien, 1965; Lee and Devore, 1968; Leroi-Gourhan, 1964b; Oakley, 1964; Piveteau, 1957; Robinson and Mason, 1957.

STONE IMPLEMENTS—MANUFACTURE

STONE TOOL MATERIALS

Crabtree, 1967; Cann and Renfrew, 1964; Dixon, Cann and Renfrew, 1968; Frondel, 1962; Goodman, 1944; Goodwin, 1960; Hurlbut, 1952; Pei, 1936; Renfrew, Dixon and Cann, 1966; Shotton, 1963; Warren, 1914.

QUARRYING

Becker, 1959; Clark, J. G. D., 1952; Grantzau, 1954; Houlder, 1961; Swanson, 1968.

CHIPPED IMPLEMENTS, GENERAL

Barnes, 1939; Barnes and Cheynier, 1935; Blacking, 1953; *Bordes,* 1947, 1961b, *1967;* Brézillon, 1968; Capitan, 1917; Catlin, 1867; Cole, 1954; Coutier, 1929; Crabtree, 1966; Edeine, 1960; Elkin, 1948; Ellis, 1940; Gould, 1968; Heinzelin de Braucourt, 1962; Hodges, 1960; Holmes, 1919; Humphreys, 1952; Jelinek, 1965; Knowles, 1944, 1953; Kroeber, 1961; Lacaille, 1940, 1947, 1954; *Leakey, L. S. B., 1954;* Leroi-Gourhan, 1943, 1964b; Leroi-Gourhan and Brézillon, 1966; Leroi-Gourhan and Others, 1966; McCarthy, 1943; McCarthy, Bramell and Noone, 1946; Mewhinney, 1957; Movius, 1941; *Oakley, 1954, 1957a,* 1957b, *1964;* Pei, 1936; Pfeiffer, 1912, 1920; Pond, 1930; Pradel, 1958; Robinson, 1938; Sankalia, 1964; Sellers, 1885; *Semenov, 1964;* Smith, P. E. L., 1966b; Sonneville-Bordes, 1967; Swanson, 1966, 1968; Tixier, 1963; Warren, 1914; Watson, 1956; Wilmsen, 1968a, 1968b; Wilson, 1899.

CHOPPERS AND BIFACES

Alimen, 1963; Baden-Powell, 1949; Barnes, 1939; Breuil and Kelley, 1956; Clark, J. D., 1958, 1963, 1966; Coghlan, 1943; Howell, 1966; Howell and J. D. Clark, 1963; Kelley, 1937; Leakey, L. S. B., 1951; Leakey, M. D., 1963; Mason, 1962; Oakley, 1957b; Ramendo, 1963; Robinson and Mason, 1957; University of California, 1967; Vértes, 1965; Walker and Sieveking, 1962.

LEVALLOIS AND MOUSTERIAN FLAKE TOOLS

Barnes and Kidder, 1936; Binford and Binford, 1966, 1969; Bordes, 1948, 1953a, 1953b, 1954, 1961a; Kelley, 1954; Taute, 1965; University of California, 1967.

BLADE TOOLS

Barnes and Cheynier, 1935; Bordes, 1965, 1967; Breuil, 1913; Cabrol and Cloutier, 1932; Chabas, 1874; Cheynier, 1958; Clark, J. G. D. and Thompson, 1965; Crabtree, 1968; Dönmez and Brice, 1951; Dreyfus, 1960; Laplace, 1966, 1968; Laplace-Jauretche, 1957; Leroi-Gourhan and Brézillon, 1966; Movius, 1966; Peyrony, 1935; Sackett, 1966; Sankalia, 1967; Smith, P. E. L., 1964, 1966a; Sonneville-Bordes, 1960; Sonneville-Bordes and Perrot, 1953, 1954, 1955, 1956a, 1956b; Taute, 1965.

MICROLITHS

Barnes, 1947; Bordes, 1957; Clark, J. G. D., 1954; Daniel and Vignard, 1953; Sanger, 1968; Sankalia, 1967.

HEAT TREATMENT

Bordes, 1967; Crabtree and Butler, 1964; Malik, 1961; Man, 1883; Robinson, 1938; Sankalia, 1967; Shippee, 1963; Squier, 1953.

GROUND IMPLEMENTS

Chappell, 1966; Clark, J. G. D., 1952; Coghlan, 1943; Cole, 1954; Grantzau, 1954; Holmes, 1919; Houlder, 1961; Iversen, 1956; Leroi-Gourhan, 1943; Leroi-Gourhan and others, 1966; Pfeiffer, 1912, 1920; Pond, 1930; Semenov, 1964; Shotton, 1963; Skinner, 1948; Sonnenfeld, 1962; Wilson, 1899.

STONE IMPLEMENTS—USES

USES, GENERAL

Biberson and Aguirre, 1965; Binford and Binford, 1966, 1969; *Bordes, 1965, 1967;* Childe, 1942; Clark, J. G. D. and Thompson, 1965; Cole, 1954; Crabtree and Davis, 1968; Edeine, 1960; Freeman & Butzer, 1966; Frison, 1968; Keller, 1966; Leakey, 1954; Movius, 1966; Pfeiffer, 1912, 1920; Pradel, 1958; *Semenov, 1964;* Smith, G. V., 1893.

HAFTING

Allain and Descouts, 1957; Becker, 1945; Cheynier, 1956; Semenov, 1964; Strahm, 1961, 1962.

IN HUNTING, FISHING AND GATHERING

Barnett, 1961; Breuil and Lantier, 1959; Garrod, 1946, 1955; Gould, 1968; Lee and Devore, 1968; Leroi-Gourhan, 1945, 1955;

Lindner, 1937; McCarthy, 1958; McCarthy, Bramell and Noone, 1946; Mitchell, 1949; Movius, 1950; Noone, 1949; Oakley, 1961; Peyrony, 1935; Pond, 1930; Pope, 1918, 1923; Profe, 1914; Sollas, 1924; Wilmsen, 1968a, 1968b; Wilson, 1899.

IN FOREST CLEARANCE AND AGRICULTURE

Clark, J. G. D., 1945, 1947, 1952, 1965; Coghlan, 1943; Darby, 1956; Iversen, 1956; Leroi-Gourhan, 1945; Skinner, 1948; Smith, G. V., 1893; Sonnenfeld, 1962.

NORTH AMERICA, ETHNOLOGICAL DATA

Catlin, 1867; Crabtree, 1968; Ellis, 1940; Frison, 1968; Holmes, 1919; Kroeber, 1961; Martin, Quimby and Collier, 1947; Moorehead, 1910, 1917; Pond, 1930; Pope, 1918, 1923; Squier, 1953; Swanson, 1968; Willey, 1966; Wormington, 1957; Wilson, 1899.

AUSTRALIA, ETHNOLOGICAL DATA

Allchin, 1957; Elkin, 1948; McCarthy, 1943, 1958; McCarthy, Bramell and Noone, 1946; Gould, 1968; Mitchell, 1949; Noone, 1949; Thompson, 1964.

OTHER AREAS, ETHNOLOGICAL DATA

Chappell, 1966; Malik, 1961; Man, 1883.

GUN FLINTS AND THRESHING

Bordaz, 1965, 1969; Clarke, 1935; Edeine, 1963; Knowles and Barnes, 1937; Luquet and Rivet, 1933; Maury, 1966; Schleicher, 1927; Skertchly, 1879.

FIRE PRODUCTION

Leroi-Gourhan, 1943; Oakley, 1956, 1961; Hough, 1926.

MISCELLANEOUS

ILLUSTRATIONS

Barnett, 1961; Bordes, 1961b, 1968; Brézillon, 1968; Déchelette, 1908; Evans, 1897; Heinzelin de Braucourt, 1962; Howell, 1959, 1965; Laplace, 1966, 1968; Laplace-Jauretche, 1957; Leroi-Gourhan, 1949; Leroi-Gourhan and others, 1966; Moorehead, 1910, 1917; Mortillet and Mortillet, 1881; Movius, 1956; Oakley, 1957a, 1964; Smith, P. E. L., 1966a; Sonneville-Bordes, 1967; Sonneville-Bordes and Perrot, 1953, 1954, 1955, 1956a, 1956b; Tixier, 1963; Watson, 1956; Willey, 1966; Wormington, 1957.

ART AND BURIALS

Bataille, 1955; Binford, S. R., 1968; Breuil, 1952; Gideon, 1962; Graziozi, 1960; Laming-Emperaire, 1962; Leroi-Gourhan, 1964a, 1965a, 1965b; Ucko and Rosenfeld, 1967.

PREHISTORIC SETTLEMENTS

Childe, 1950; Clark, J. D., 1966; Howell, 1966; Howell and J. D. Clark, 1963; Klima, 1954; Leroi-Gourhan, 1965a; Leroi-Gourhan and Brézillon, 1966.

PHOTOGRAPHY OF STONE TOOLS, METHODS

Déribéré, Porchez and Tendron, 1951; Lewis, 1960; MacDonald and Sanger, 1968; Swanson, 1966; Tendron, 1949.

MOTION PICTURES ON STONE KNAPPING

Leechman, 1950; Swanson, 1968; University of California, 1967.

Bibliography

Alimen, Henriette
1965   *Atlas de préhistoire, vol. 1, généralités, méthodes en pré-histoire,* 2nd ed., Paris, Boubée & Cie., 185 pp.
1955   *Préhistoire de l'Afrique,* 1957. Transl. by A. H. Brodrick "The prehistory of Africa," London, Hutchinson, 438 pp.
1963   Enclumes (percuteurs dormants) associés à l'Acheuléen supérieur de l'Ougartien. *Bulletin de la Société Préhistorique Française,* vol. 40, no. 1–2, pp. 43–47.

Allain, J., and J. Descouts
1957   A propos d'une baguette à rainure armée de silex découverte dans le Magdalénien de Saint-Marcel. *L'Anthropologie,* vol. 61, no. 5–6. pp. 503–12.

Allchin, Bridget
1957   Australian Stone Industries past and present. *Journal of the Royal Anthropological Institute,* vol. 87, pp. 115–36.

Baden-Powell, D. F. W.
1949   Experimental clactonian technique. *Proceedings of the Prehistoric Society,* vol. 15, pp. 38–41.

Bailloud, G., and P. Mieg de Boofzheim
1955   *Les civilisations néolithiques de la France dans leur con-
          texte Européen.* Paris, A. and J. Picard & Cie., xv, 244 pp.
Balout, L.
1955   *Préhistoire de l'Afrique du Nord; essai de chronologie.*
          Paris, Arts et Métiers Graphiques, 544 pp.
Barnes, Alfred S.
1939   The differences between natural and human flaking on
          prehistoric stone implements. *American Anthropologist,*
          vol. 41, no. 1, pp. 99–112.
1947   The technique of blade production in mesolithic and neo-
          lithic times. *Proceedings of the Prehistoric Society,* vol.
          13, pp. 101–13.
Barnes, Alfred S., and André Cheynier
1935   Etude sur les techniques de débitage du silex et en par-
          ticulier des nuclei prismatiques. *Bulletin de la Société
          Préhistorique Française,* vol. 32, pp. 288–99.
Barnes, Alfred S., and H. H. Kidder
1936   Différentes techniques de débitage à la Ferrassie. *Bulletin
          de la Société Préhistorique Française,* vol. 33, pp. 272–88.
Barnett, Lincoln
1961   *The epic of man.* New York, Time Inc., 307 pp.
Bataille, Georges
1955   *Lascaux ou la naissance de l'art.* Genève, Skira, 151 pp.
Becker, C. J.
1945   New finds of hafted Neolithic celts. *Acta Archaeologica,*
          vol. 16, Copenhagen, pp. 156–75.
1959   Flint mining in Neolithic Denmark, *Antiquity,* vol. 33,
          pp. 87–92.
Biberson, Pierre, and Emiliano Aguirre
1965   Expériences de taille d'outils préhistoriques dans des os
          d'éléphant. *Quaternaria,* vol. 7, pp. 165–82.
Bibby, Geoffrey
1956   *The testimony of the spade.* New York, Knopf, 411 pp.
Binford, Lewis R.
1968   Post-Pleistocene adaptations. in: Binford S. R., and L. R.
          Binford *New perspectives in archaeology,* Chicago, Aldine
          Publishing Company, pp. 313–41.
Binford, Lewis R., and Sally R. Binford
1966   *A preliminary analysis of functional variability in the
          Mousterian of Levallois facies.* In J. D. Clark and F. C.

Howell (eds.). Recent studies in paleoanthropology. *American Anthropologist,* vol. 68, no. 2, part 2, 394 pp.

Binford, Sally R.
1968 A structural comparison of disposal of the dead in the Mousterian and Upper Paleolithic. *Southwestern Journal of Anthropology,* vol. 24, no. 2, pp. 139–54.

Binford, Sally R., and Lewis R. Binford
1969 Stone tools and human behavior. *Scientific American,* vol. 220, no. 4, pp. 70–84.

Bishop, Walter M., and J. Desmond Clark (eds.)
1963 *Background to evolution in Africa.* Chicago, University of Chicago Press, 935 pp.

Blacking, John
1953 Edward Simpson, alias "Flint Jack." A Victorian craftsman. *Antiquity,* vol. 27, pp. 207–11.

Bohmers, A.
1963 A statistical analysis of flint artifacts. In Don Brothwell and Eric Higgs, eds., *Science in Archaeology.* New York, Basic Books, 595 pp.

Bordaz, Jacques
1959a First tools of mankind, *Natural History,* vol. 68, pp. 36–51.
1959b The new stone age. *Natural History,* vol. 68, pp. 92–101.
1965 The threshing sledge. *Natural History,* vol. 74, pp. 26–29.
1969 Flint flaking in Turkey. *Natural History,* vol. 78, pp. 73–79.

Bordes, François
1947 Etude comparative des différentes techniques de taille du silex et des roches dures. *L'Anthropologie,* vol. 51, pp. 1–29.

1948 Les couches moustériennes du gisement du Moustier (Dordogne) Typologie et technique de taille. *Bulletin de la Société Préhistorique Française,* vol. 45, pp. 113–25.

1950 Principes d'une méthode d'étude des techniques de débitage et de la typologie du paléolithique ancien et moyen. *L'Anthropologie,* vol. 54, pp. 19–34.

1953a Notules de typologie paléolithique. I. Outils moustériens à fracture volontaire. *Bulletin de la Société Préhistorique Française,* vol. 50, pp. 224–26.

1953b (Same title). II. Pointes levaloisiennes et pointes pseudo-levaloisiennes. *Ibid.,* vol. 50, pp. 311–13.

1954 (Same title). III. Pointes moustériennes, racloirs convergents et déjetés, limaces. *Ibid.,* vol. 51, pp. 336–39.

1957   La signification du microburin dans le paléolithique supérieur. *L'Anthropologie,* Paris, vol. 61, pp. 578–82.

1961a   Mousterian cultures in France. *Science,* vol. 134, pp. 803–10.

1961b   *Typologie du paléolithique ancien et moyen.* Publications de l'Institut de Préhistoire, Université de Bordeaux, mémoire no. 1, 2 vols., Bordeaux, imprimerie Delmas, 86 pp., figs., and vol. of plates.

1965   Utilisation possible des côtés de burins. *Fundberichte aus Schwaben,* vol. 17, pp. 3-4.

1967   Considérations sur la typologie et les techniques dans le paléolithique. *Quartär,* vol. 18, pp. 25–55, 8 pls.

1968   *The old stone age.* New York, McGraw-Hill. 255pp.

Brace, C. Loring
1967   *The stages of human evolution: human and cultural origins.* Englewood Cliffs, Prentice-Hall, 116 pp.

Brace, C. Loring, and M. F. Ashley Montagu
1965   *Man's evolution. An introduction to physical anthropology.* New York, The Macmillan Company, 352 pp.

Braidwood, Robert J.
1967   *Prehistoric men.* 7th. ed. Glenview, Illinois, Scott, Foresman and Co., 181 pp.

Braidwood, Robert J., and Bruce Howe
1957   *Prehistoric investigations in Iraqi Kurdistan. Studies in ancient oriental civilization,* no. 31. Chicago, University of Chicago Press, 184 pp., 29 plates.

Breuil, Henri
1913   *Les subdivisions du paléolithique supérieur et leur signification:* Compte Rendu, 14th Session, vol. 1, Congrès International d'Anthropologie et d'Archéologie Préhistorique, Geneva, 1912, pp. 165–238. 1937. 2nd ed. Lagny.

1952   *Four hundred centuries of cave art.* Translated from the French edition, 1952, by M. E. Boyle. Montignac, Centre d'étude et de documentation préhistorique. 413 pp.

Breuil, Henri, and Raymond Lantier
1959   *Les hommes de la Pierre ancienne (paléolithique et mésolithique).* 2nd ed. rev. Paris, Payot, 360 pp.

Breuil, Henri, and Harper Kelley
1956   Les éclats acheuléens à plan de frappe à facettes de Cagny-la-Garenne (Somme). *Bulletin de la Société Préhistorique Française,* vol. 53, pp. 174–91.

Brézillon, Michel N.
1968   La dénomination des objects de pierre taillée. Matériaux pour un vocabulaire des préhistoriens de langue française. Supplément IV, *Gallia Préhistoire,* 413 pp.

Brothwell, D., and E. Higgs (eds.)
1963   *Science in archaeology.* New York, Basic Books, 595 pp.

Butzer, Karl W.
1964   *Environment and archeology. An introduction to pleistocene geography.* Chicago, Aldine Publishing Company. 524 pp.
1965   Physical conditions in eastern Europe, western Asia and Egypt before the period of agricultural and urban settlement. *Cambridge Ancient History,* Revised edition, vol. IV, chap. II, fascicle 33, New York, Cambridge University Press, 39 pp.

Cabrol, Alexis, and L. Coutier
1932   Contribution à l'étude de la taille de l'obsidienne au Mexique. *Bulletin de la Société Préhistorique Française,* vol. 29, pp. 579–582.

Cann, J. R., and Colin Renfrew
1964   The characterization of obsidian and its application to the Mediterranean region. *Proceedings of the Prehistoric Society,* vol. 30, pp. 111–13.

Capitan, Louis
1917   Origine et mode de fabrication des principaux types d'armes et outils en pierre. *Revue Anthropologique,* vol. 27, pp. 1–51.

Cartailhac, Emile
1877   *L'âge de pierre dans les souvenirs et superstitions populaires.* Paris, C. Reinwald & Cie., 103 pp.

Catlin, George
1867   *Last rambles amongst the Indians of the Rocky Mountains and the Andes.* New York, D. Appleton and Company, 361 pp.

Chabas, François
1874   *Les silex de Volgu (Saône & Loire).* Chalon-sur-Saône, Société d'Histoire et d'Archéologie de Chalon-sur-Saône. 24 pp.

Chang, Kwang-Chih
1963a   *The archaeology of Ancient China.* New Haven, Yale
         University Press. 346 pp., illus., maps.
1963b   Prehistoric archaeology in China; 1920–60. *Arctic Anthro-
         pology,* vol. 1, no. 2, pp. 29–61.
1968   Archeology of ancient China. *Science,* vol. 162, pp. 519–26.

Chappell, J.
1966   Stone axe factories in the highlands of east New Guinea.
         Proceedings of the Prehistoric Society, vol. 32, pp. 96–121.

Charlesworth, John Kaye
1957   *The quaternary era; with special reference to its glaciation.*
         London, E. Arnold, 2 vols., 1700 pp.

Cheynier, André
1956   Feuille de laurier emmanchée à Badegoule. *Bulletin de la
         Société Préhistorique Française,* vol. 53, pp. 94–95.
1958   Impromptu sur la séquence des pointes du Paléolithique
         supérieur. *Bulletin de la Société Préhistorique Française,*
         vol. 55, pp. 190–205.

Childe, V. Gordon
1941   *Man makes himself.* New York, Mentor books, 192 pp.
1942   The antiquity and function of antler axes and adzes.
         Antiquity, vol. 16, p. 258.
1950   Cave men's buildings. *Antiquity,* Gloucester, vol. 24, pp.
         4–11.
1956   The new stone age. In Shapiro, Harry L. (ed.), *Man,
         culture, and society.* New York, Oxford University Press,
         pp. 94–110.

Clark, John Desmond
1958   The natural fracture of pebbles from the Batoka Gorge,
         Northern Rhodesia, and its bearing on the Kafuan in-
         dustries of Africa. *Proceedings of the Prehistoric Society,*
         vol. 24, pp. 64–77.
1959   *The prehistory of Southern Africa.* Harmondsworth,
         Middlesex Penguin Books, 341 pp.
1960   Human ecology during Pleistocene and later times in Africa
         south of the Sahara. *Current Anthropology,* vol. 1, no.
         4, pp. 307–24.
1963   The problem of the pebble cultures. 6th International Con-
         gress of Prehistoric and Protohistoric Sciences. Rome, vol.
         I, pp. 265–71.
1966   Acheulian occupation sites in the Middle East and Africa:

a study in cultural variability. In J. D. Clark, and F. C. Howell (eds.). Recent studies in paleoanthropology. *American Anthropologist,* vol. 68, no. 2, part 2, 394 pp.

1967   *An atlas of African prehistory.* London, Cambridge University Press, 12 maps, 38 overlays.

Clark, John Desmond, and F. Clark Howell (eds.)
1966   Recent studies in palaeoanthropology. *American Anthropologist,* vol. 68, no. 2, part 2, 394 pp.

Clark, John Grahame D.
1936   *The mesolithic settlement of northern Europe.* Cambridge, The University Press, xvi, 283 pp.

1945   Farmers and forests in neolithic Europe. *Antiquity,* vol. 19, pp. 57–71.

1947   Forest clearance and prehistoric farming. *Economic History Review,* vol. 17, pp. 45–51.

1952   *Prehistoric Europe. The economic basis.* London, Methuen Co., 349 pp.

1954   *Excavations at Star Carr.* Cambridge, the University Press, 220 pp.

1957   *Archaeology and society.* Cambridge, Harvard University Press, 272 pp.

1961   *World prehistory, an outline.* Cambridge, the University Press, 284 pp., illus.

1962   A survey of the Mesolithic phase in the prehistory of Europe and South-West Asia. *6th International Congress of Prehistoric and Protohistoric Sciences.* Rome, vol. 1, pp. 97–111.

1965   Radiocarbon dating and the expansion of farming cultures from the Near East. Cambridge, *Proceedings of the Prehistoric Society,* vol. 31, pp. 58–73.

1967   *The stone age hunters.* New York, McGraw-Hill, 143 pp.

Clark, John Grahame D., and S. Piggott
1965   *Prehistoric societies.* London, Hutchison, 356 pp.

Clark, John Grahame D., and M. W. Thompson
1965   The groove and splinter technique of working antler in Upper Palaeolithic and Mesolithic Europe. *Proceedings of the Prehistoric Society,* Cambridge, England, vol. 19, pp. 148–60.

Clark, Wilfrid LeGros
1964   *The fossil evidence for human evolution: an introduction to the study of Paleoanthropology.* 2nd edition. Chicago,

University of Chicago Press, 200 pp.

1967   *Man-apes or ape-men?* New York, Holt, Rinehart and Winston, 150 pp.

Clarke, Rainbird

1935   The flint knapping industry at Brandon. *Antiquity,* vol. 9, pp. 38–56.

Coghlan, H. H.

1943   The evolution of the axe from prehistoric to Roman times. *Journal of the Royal Anthropological Institute,* vol. 73, pt. 1 and 2, pp. 27–56.

Cole, Sonia M.

1954   Differentiation of non-metallic tools. In Singer, Holmyard, and Hall (eds.), A history of technology. Oxford, Clarendon Press, vol. 1, pp. 495–519.

1963   *The prehistory of East Africa.* New York, The Macmillan Company, 382 pp., ill., maps.

Coon, Carleton S.

1962a   *The origin of races.* New York, Alfred A. Knopf; 724 pp., index.

1962b   *The story of man; from the first human to primitive culture and beyond.* New York, Knopf, 438 pp., ill.

Coutier, Léon

1929   Expériences de taille pour rechercher les anciennes techniques paléolithiques. *Bulletin de la Société Préhistorique Française,* vol. 26, pp. 172–74.

Crabtree, Donald E.

1966   A stoneworker's approach to analysing and replicating the Lindenmeier Folsom. *Tebiwa, the Journal of the Idaho State University Museum,* vol. 9, no. 1, pp. 3–39.

1967   Notes on experiments in flint knapping: 3. The flint-knapper's raw materials. *Tebiwa, the Journal of the Idaho State University Museum,* vol. 10, no. 1, pp. 8–25.

1968   Mesoamerican polyhedral cores and prismatic blades. *American Antiquity,* vol. 33, no. 4, pp. 446–78.

Crabtree, Donald E., and Robert B. Butler

1964   Notes on experiments in flint knapping: 1. Heat treatment of silica materials. *Tebiwa, the Journal of the Idaho State University Museum,* vol. 7, no. 1, pp. 1–6.

Crabtree, Donald E., and E. L. Davis

1968   Experimental manufacture of wooden implements with tools of flaked stone. *Science,* vol. 159, no. 3813, pp. 426–28.

Daniel, Glyn E.
1950   A *hundred years of archaeology.* London, Gerald Duckworth & Co., Ltd., 344 pp.
1964   *The idea of prehistory.* Baltimore, Penguin, 186 pp.
1967   *The origins and growth of archaeology.* Baltimore, New York, Thomas Y. Crowell.

Daniel, R., and E. Vignard
1953   Tableaux synoptiques des principaux microlithes géométriques du Tardenoisien français. *Bulletin de la Société Préhistorique Française,* vol. 50, pp. 314–22, 5 figs.

Darby, H. C.
1956   The clearing of the woodland in Europe. In Thomas, William L., Jr. (ed.), *Man's role in changing the face of the earth.* Chicago, University of Chicago Press, pp. 183–216.

Dechelette, Joseph
1908   *Manuel d'archéologie préhistorique, celtique et galloromaine. Archéologie préhistorique.* Paris, A. Picard & fils., vol. 1, xix, 743 pp.

Day, Michael H.
1965   *Guide to fossil man. A handbook of human palaeontology.* London, Cassell, 289 pp.

Déribéré, M., J. Porchez, and G. Tendron
1951   *La photographie scientifique.* Paris, Paul Montel, 127 pp.

Dixon, J. E., J. R. Cann, and Colin Renfrew
1968   Obsidian and the origin of trade. *Scientific American,* vol. 218, no. 3, pp. 38–44.

Dönmez, Ahmet, and W. C. Brice
1951   A flint blade workshop near Gaziantep, South Turkey. *Man,* vol. 51, pp. 76–77.

Dreyfus, M. C.
1960   Précisions sur l'outillage du Néolithique à l'âge du Bronze. *Bulletin de la Société Préhistorique Française,* vol. 30, pp. 111–13.

Dyson, Robert H., Jr.
1964   On the origins of the neolithic revolution. *Science,* vol. 144, pp. 672–75.

Edeine, Bernard

1960   Essai de contribution aux études de technologie de l'outillage néolithique. *Bulletin de la Société Préhistorique Française,* vol. 57, pp. 229–32.

1963   A propos de pierres à fusil. *Bulletin de la Société Préhistorique Française,* vol. 60, pp. 16–18.

Ehrich, R. W. (ed.)

1965   *Chronologies in Old World archaeology.* Chicago, University of Chicago Press, 557 pp.

Elkin, Adolphus P.

1948   Pressure flaking in the northern Kimberley, Australia. *Man,* London, vol. 48, pp. 110–13.

Ellis, H. Holmes

1940   *Flint working techniques of the American Indians: an experimental study.* Columbus, Ohio Historical Society, 78 pp.

Evans, John

1897   *The Ancient Stone implements, weapons, and ornaments of Great Britain,* 2nd ed., rev. London, Longmans, Green & Co., 747 pp.

Evernden, J. F., and G. H. Curtis and others

1965   The origin of man. *Current Anthropology,* vol. 6, no. 4, pp. 343–431.

Flannery, Kent V.

1965   The ecology of early food production in Mesopotamia. *Science,* vol. 147, pp. 1247–56.

Flint, Richard Foster

1957   *Glacial and Pleistocene geology.* New York, John Wiley & Sons, 553 pp.

Frison, George C.

1968   A functional analysis of certain chipped stone tools. *American Antiquity,* vol. 33, no. 2, pp. 149–55.

Freeman, L. G., Jr., and K. W. Butzer

1966   The Acheulian station of Torralba (Spain): a progress report. *Quaternaria,* vol. 8, pp. 9–21.

Frondel, Clifford

1962   *The system of mineralogy of James Dwight Dana and Edward Salisbury Dana, Yale University 1837–1892. Seventh Edition, vol. III. Silica minerals.* New York, John Wiley and Sons, 334 pp.

Gabel, W. C.
1958a   The Mesolithic continuum in Western Europe. *American*
1958b   European secondary Neolithic cultures. London, *Journal of the Royal Anthropological Institute,* vol. 62, pp. 257–69. *Anthropologist,* vol. 60, no. 4, pp. 658–67.

Garrod, D. A. E.
1946   *Environment, tools, and man.* Cambridge, The University Press, 30 pp.
1955   Paleolithic spear-throwers. *Proceedings of the Prehistoric Society,* vol. 21, pp. 21–35.

Garrod, Dorothy A. E., and J. G. D. Clark
1965   Primitive man in Egypt, Western Asia and Europe in palaeolithic and mesolithic times. *Cambridge Ancient History,* vol. 1, chap. III, New York, Cambridge University Press, 15 figs., 61 pp. Revised edition, fascicle 30.

Gideon, S.
1962   *The eternal present: the beginning of art.* New York, Bollingen Foundation, 588 pp.

Goodman, Mary Ellen
1944   The physical properties of stone tool materials. *American Antiquity,* vol. 9, no. 4, pp. 415–33.

Goodwin, A. J. H.
1953   *Method in prehistory.* 2nd edition, Cape Town, The South African Archaeological Society. Handbook Series no. 1, 188 pp.
1960   Chemical alteration (patination) of stone. In *The application of quantitative methods to archaeology,* Robert F. Heizer and Sherburne Cook (eds.). Viking Fund Publications in Anthropology, no. 28, Chicago, Quadrangle Books, pp. 300–24.

Gould, Richard A.
1968   Chipping stones in the outback. *Natural History,* vol. 77, no. 2, pp. 42–49.

Grantzau, Sylvest
1954   Stenalderens Grubedrift (Stone Age Mining). *Kulm,* Universitets-forlaget i Aarhus, pp. 30–49.

Graziozi, P.
1960   *Palaeolithic Art.* New York, McGraw-Hill, 278 pp.

128 *Bibliography*

Harlan, Jack R., and Daniel Zohari
1966   Distribution of wild wheats and barley. Washington, *Science,* vol. 153, pp. 1074–80.

Heinzelin de Braucourt, Jean de
1962   *Manuel de typologie des industries lithiques.* Bruxelles, Institut Royal des Sciences Naturelles de Belgique, 74 pp., 50 plates.

Heizer, R. F., and S. F. Cook
1960   *The application of quantitative method in archaeology.* Viking Fund Publications in Archaeology, no. 28, Chicago, Quadrangle books, 358 pp., pl., tables.

Hodges, Henri W.
1960   *Artifacts: an introduction to early materials and technology.* New York, Humanities Press.

Hole, F., and R. F. Heizer
1964   *An introduction to prehistoric archaeology.* New York, Holt, Rinehart and Winston, 306 pp.

Holmes, W. H.
1919   Handbook of aboriginal American antiquities. Part I. Introductory: The lithic industries. *Bureau of American Ethnology, Smithsonian Institution Bulletin 60,* 380 pp.

Hough, Walter
1926   Fire as an agent in human culture. *Smithsonian Institution, U. S. National Museum, Bulletin 139,* 270 pp.

Houlder, C. H.
1961   The excavation of a Neolithic stone implement factory on Mynydd Rhiw in Caernarvonshire. *Proceedings of the Prehistoric Society,* vol. 27, pp. 108–143.

Howell, F. Clark
1959   Upper pleistocene stratigraphy and early man in the Levant. *Proceedings of the American Philosophical Society,* vol. 103:1.

1964   The hominization process. In *Horizons of anthropology,* Sol Tax ed., Chicago, Aldine Publishing Company, pp. 49–59.

1965   *Early Man.* New York, Time Inc., 200 pp., illustrated.
1966   Observations on the earlier phases of the European lower palaeolithic. In: Recent studies in palaeoanthropology, edited by J. Desmond Clark and F. Clark Howell. *American Anthropologist,* Menasha, vol. 68, pt. 2, no. 2, pp. 88–201.

Howell, F. Clark, and F. Bourlière (eds.)

1963   *African ecology and human evolution.* Viking Fund Publications in Anthropology, no. 36, Chicago, Aldine Publishing Company, 666 pp.

Howell, F. Clark, and J. Desmond Clark

1963   Acheulian hunters-gatherers of sub-Saharan Africa. In *F. C. Howell and F. Bourlière,* (eds.) African ecology and human evolution. Viking Fund Publications in Anthropology, no. 36, Chicago, Aldine Publishing Company, 666 pp.

Howells, William

1967   *Mankind in the making: the story of human evolution.* Garden City, Doubleday & Co.

Humphreys, H.

1952   Flint tools and their makers. *Antiquity,* vol. 26, pp. 123–34.

Hurlbut, Cornelius S., Jr.

1952   *Dana's manual of mineralogy. Sixteenth Edition.* New York, John Wiley and Sons, 530 pp., illus.

Ikawa, Fumiko

1968   Some aspects of Palaeolithic cultures in Japan. In *La Préhistoire. Problèmes et tendances.* Paris, Centre National de la Recherche Scientifique, pp. 237–44.

Iversen, Johannes

1956   Forest clearance in the stone age. *Scientific American,* vol. 194, pp. 36–41.

Jelinek, Arthur J.

1965   Lithic Technology conference. *American Antiquity,* vol. 31, no. 2, part 1, pp. 277–79.

Jullien, R.

1965   *Les hommes fossiles de la pierre taillée.* Paris, Boubée, 363 pp., ill.

Jussieu, Antoine de

1725   De l'origine et des usages de la pierre de foudre. *Histoire de l'Académie Royale des Sciences* 1723, Mémoires. Paris, pp. 6–9.

Keller, Charles M.

1966   The development of edge damage patterns on stone tools. *Man,* vol. 1, no. 4, pp. 501–11.

Kelley, Harper
1937   Acheulian flake tools. *Proceedings of the Prehistoric Society,* vol. 3, pp. 15–29.
1954   Contribution à l'étude de la technique de la taille levaloisienne. *Bulletin de la Société Préhistorique Française,* vol. 51, pp. 149–69, 13 figs.

Klima, Bohuslav
1954   Paleolithic huts at Dolní Věstonice, Czechoslovakia. *Antiquity,* vol. 28, pp. 4–14.

Klindt-Jensen, Ole
1957   *Denmark before the Vikings.* New York, Praeger, 212 pp.

Knowles, Francis H. S.
1944   The manufacture of a flint arrow-head by quartzite hammerstone. *Occasional Papers on Technology, no. 1, Pitt Rivers Museum. Oxford University,* 37 pp.
1953   Stone worker's progress. *Ibid.,* no. 6, 120 pp.

Knowles, Francis H. S., and Alfred S. Barnes
1937   Manufacture of gunflints. *Antiquity,* vol. 11, no. 42, (Notes and News), pp. 201–7.

Kroeber, Theodora
1961   *Ishi in two worlds. A biography of the last wild Indian in North America.* Berkeley, University of California Press, 258 pp.

Lacaille, A. D.
1940   Aspects of intentional fracture. *Transactions of the Glasgow Archaeological Society,* vol. 9, pp. 314–41.
1947   The scraper in prehistoric culture. *Ibid.,* vol. 11, pp. 38–93.
1954   Stone age tools. *Ibid.,* vol. 13, pp. 17–32.

Laming-Emperaire, A.
1963   *L'Archéologie préhistorique.* Paris, Editions du Seuil, 192 pp.
1962   *La signification de l'art paléolithique.* Paris, A. and J. Picard, 424 pp.
1964   *Origines de l'archéologie préhistorique en France. Des superstitions médiévales à la découverte de l'homme fossile.* Paris, A. and J. Picard, 244 pp.

Laplace, George
1966   Recherches sur l'origine et l'évolution des complexes

leptolithiques. *Ecole Française de Rome, Mélanges d'arché-ologie et d'histoire, supplément no. 4,* Paris, E. de Boc-card, 586 pp., 25 plates.

1968   Recherches de typologie analytique 1968. In *Origini II. Preistoria e Protostoria delle Civilta' antiche.* Rome, Instituto di Paletnologia, pp. 7–60.

Laplace-Jauretche, George
1957   Typologie analytique. Application d'une nouvelle méthode d'étude des formes et des structures aux industries à lames et à lamelles. *Quaternaria,* vol. 4, pp. 133–64.

Lavocat, R. and others
1966   Faunes et flores préhistoriques de l'Europe occidentale. "L'Homme et ses origines," in: Alimen H., *Atlas de pré-histoire, Vol. 3,* Paris, Boubée.

Leakey, L. S. B.
1951   *Olduvai Gorge.* Cambridge, Cambridge University Press, 164 pp.

1954   *Working stone, bone and wood.* In Singer, Charles, E. J. Holmyard, and A. R. Hall (eds.), A history of technology. Vol. I, from early times to fall of ancient empires. New York and London, Oxford University Press, pp. 128–43.

Leakey, M. D.
1963   *Preliminary survey of the cultural material from Beds I and II, Olduvai Gorge, Tanzania.* In Bishop, Walter M., and J. Desmond Clark, (eds.), Background to evolution in Africa. Chicago, University of Chicago Press, 935 pp.

Lee, Richard B., and Irven Devore (eds.)
1968   *Man the hunter.* Chicago, Aldine, 384 pp. Of special in-terest are the discussions and articles in Part V, demography and population ecology, Part VI, prehistoric hunters and gatherers, Part VII, hunting and human population, pp. 219–346.

Leechman, Douglas
1950   *Making primitive stone tools.* National Film Board of Canada. Black and white, sound, 11 minutes long.

Leroi-Gourhan, André
1943   *L'homme et la matière.* Paris, Albin Michel, 367 pp.
1945   *Milieu et techniques.* Paris, Albin Michel, 512 pp.
1949   La préhistoire. *La documentation photographique. Série no. 10.* Paris, Documentation Française, 12 pp., 11 pls.

1955   *Les hommes de la préhistoire*. Les Chasseurs, Paris, Bourrelier. 1957. English Transl., *"Prehistoric men,"* New York, Philosophical Library, 120 pp.

1964a   *Les religions de la préhistoire (Paléolithique)*. Paris, Presses Universitaires de France, 154 pp.

1964b   *Le geste et la parole. Technique et langage*. Paris, Albin Michel, 323 pp.

1965a   *Le geste et la parole. La mémoire et les rythmes*. Paris, Albin Michel, 285 pp.

1965b   *Préhistoire de l'art occidental*. Paris, Editions d'art Lucien Mazenod, 482 pp., 803 ill.

Leroi-Gourhan A. et M. Brézillon
1966   Habitation magdalénienne no. 1 de Pincevent près Montereau (Seine-et-Marne). *Gallia Préhistoire*, C. N. R. S., tome IX, fascicule 2, pp. 263–385.

Leroi-Gourhan, André and others
1966   *La préhistoire*. Collection Nouvelle Clio, no. 1. Paris, Presses Universitaires de France. 366 pp. See especially: Terminologie de la pierre et de l'os by A. Leroi-Gourhan, pp. 241–71.

Lewis, T. W.
1960   Projectile point photography. *Tennessee Archaeologist*, vol. 16, no. 1, pp. 43–45.

Lindner, Kurt
1937   *Die Jagd der Vorzeit*. 1941. Transl. from the German by G. Montandon *"La chasse préhistorique."* Paris, Payot, 480 pp.

Lubbock, John (Lord Avebury).
1913   *Pre-historic times*. 7th ed. London, Williams & Norgate, New York, Henry Holt, 623 pp.

Lumley, Henry de
1969   A Paleolithic Camp at Nice. *Scientific American,* vol. 220, no. 5, pp 42–50.

Luquet, G., and P. Rivet
1933   Sur le tribulum. *Mélanges offerts à Mr. Nicolas Iorga par ses amis de France et des pays de langue française*. Paris, Librairie Universitaire, J. Gamber, pp. 613–39.

McBurney, Charles B. M.
1950   The geographical study of the older Palaeolithic stages in Europe. *Proceedings of the Prehistoric Society*, Cambridge, England, vol. 16, pp. 163–83.

1960   *The stone age of Northern Africa.* Harmondsworth, Middlesex, Penguin Books, 288 pp.

McCarthy, Frederick D.
1943   An analysis of the knapped implements from eight "elouera" industry stations on the south coast of New South Wales. *Records of the Australian Museum, Sydney,* vol. 21, pp. 127–153.
1958   *Australian aborigines; their life and culture.* Melbourne, Colorgravure Publications, 200 pp.

McCarthy, Frederick D., E. Bramell, and H. V. V. Noone
1946   The stone implements of Australia. *Australian Museum, Memoir 9,* pp. 1–94.

MacDonald, G., and D. Sanger
1968   Some aspects of microscope and photomicrography of lithic artifacts. *American Antiquity,* vol. 33, no. 2, pp. 237–40.

Malik, S. C.
1961   Stone age techniques in nineteenth-century India. *Man,* vol. 61, p. 163.

Man, E. H.
1883   Stone implements. In On the aboriginal inhabitants of the Andaman islands. *Journal of the Anthropological Institute* of Great Britain & Ireland, vol. 12, pp. 379–81.

Martin, Paul S., George I. Quimby, and Donald Collier
1947   Chap. 4. Objects of Stone. In *Indians before Columbus.* University of Chicago Press, pp. 29–39.

Mason, Revil
1962   *Prehistory of the Transvaal.* Johannesburg, Witwatersrand University Press, 498 pp.

Maury, R.
1966   Industrie de la pierre à fusil, dernière héritière des techniques de la préhistoire. *Science et Progrès. La Nature,* no. 3375, pp. 267–70.

Mellaart, James
1965   *Earliest civilizations of the Near East.* New York, McGraw-Hill, 143 pp.

Mewhinney, H.
1957   *A manual for Neanderthals.* Austin, University of Texas Press, 122 pp.

Mitchell, Stanley
1949   *Stone-age craftsmen.* Melbourne, Tait Book Co., 211 pp.

134 *Bibliography*

Moorehead, Warren K.

1910　*The stone age in North America.* Boston, Houghton Mifflin Co., 2 vols., 457 pp. and 417 pp.

1917　*Stone ornaments used by Indians in the United States and Canada.* Andover, Mass., Andover Press, 448 pp.

Mortillet, Gabriel de, and Adrien de Mortillet

1881　*Musée préhistorique.* Paris, C. Reinwald, 100 pls., 1269 figs., (1903, 2nd ed. rev.).

1900　*Le préhistorique, origine et antiquité de l'homme.* 3rd ed. Paris, Schleicher Frères, 709 pp.

Movius, Hallam L., Jr.

1941　Review of "Flint-working techniques of the American Indians: an experimental study," by H. H. Ellis, *American Antiquity,* vol. 6, pp. 369–70.

1944　Early man and Pleistocene stratigraphy in southern and eastern Asia. *Papers Peabody Museum of American Archaeology and Ethnology,* Harvard Univ., vol. 19, no. 3, pp. 1–125.

1949a　The lower palaeolithic cultures of southern and eastern Asia. *Transactions of the American Philosophical Society,* vol. 38, pp. 329–420.

1949b　Old world palaeolithic archaeology. *Bulletin of the Geological Society,* vol. 60, pp. 1443–56.

1949c　Lower paleolithic archaeology in Southern Asia and the Far East. In Early Man in the Far East. *Studies in Physical Anthropology, no. 1. American Association of Physical Anthropologists,* pp. 17–98.

1950　A wooden spear of third interglacial age from lower Saxony. *Southwestern Journal of Anthropology,* vol. 6, pp. 139–42.

1956　The old stone age. In Shapiro, Harry L., (ed.), *Man, culture, and society.* New York, Oxford University Press, pp. 49–93.

1966　Histoire de la reconnaissance des burins en silex et de la découverte de leur fonction en tant qu'outils pendant le Paléolithique Supérieur. *Bulletin de la Société Préhistorique Française,* LXIII, no. 1, pp. 50–65.

Mulvaney, D. J.

1961　The stone age of Australia. *Proceedings of the Prehistoric Society,* vol. 27, pp. 56–107.

1965　The prehistory of the Australian aborigines. New York, *Scientific American,* vol. 214, no. 3, pp. 84–93.

Noone, H. V. V.
1949   Some implements of the Australian aborigines with European parallels. *Man,* vol. 49, no. 146, pp. 111–14.

Oakley, Kenneth P.
1954   Skill as a human possession. In Singer, Holmyard, and Hall (eds.), *A history of technology.* Oxford University Press, vol. I, pp. 1–37.
1956   Fire as a Paleolithic tool and weapon. *Proceedings of the Prehistoric Society,* 1955, vol. 21, pp. 36–48.
1957a   *Man the toolmaker.* 3rd ed. Phoenix Books. University of Chicago Press, 159 pp.
1957b   Tools makyth man. *Antiquity,* vol. 31, pp. 199–209.
1961   On man's use of fire, with comments on tool-making and hunting. In *Social life of early man,* Sherwood L. Washburn, ed. Viking Fund Publication, no. 31, New York, Wenner-Gren Foundation for Anthropological Research, Inc., 176–93.
1964   *Frameworks for dating fossil man.* Chicago, Aldine Publishing Company, 355 pp.

Pei, Wen Chung
1936   Le rôle des phénomènes naturels dans l'éclatement et le façonnement des roches dures utilisées par l'homme préhistorique. *Revue de Géographie Physique et de Géologie Dynamique,* vol. 9, pp. 347–423.

Peyrony, D.
1935   Le gisement Castanet, vallon de Castermerle, commune de Sergeac (Dordogne); Aurignacien I et II. *Bulletin de la Société Préhistorique Française,* tome 23, pp. 418–43.
1948   *Eléments de Préhistoire.* Paris, A. Costes, 5th ed., 182 pp.

Pfeiffer, Ludwig
1912   *Die steinzeitliche Technik und ihre Beziehungen zur Gegenwart.* Jena, Gustav Fischer, 340 pp.
1920   *Die Werkzeuge des Steinzeit-Menschen.* Jena, Gustav Fischer, 415 pp.

Piggott, Stuart
1965   *Ancient Europe, from the beginnings of agriculture to classical antiquity; a survey.* Chicago, Aldine Publishing Company, 343 pp., illus., maps.

Piveteau, Jean
1957   *Traité de paléontologie, vol. 7, vers la forme humaine, le*

problème biologique de l'homme, les époques de l'intelli-gence. Primates, paléontologie humaine. Paris, Masson, 675 pp.

Pond, Alonzo W.
1930   Primitive methods of working stone. Based on experi-ments of Halvor L. Skavlem. Beloit, Wis., *Logan Museum Bulletin,* vol. 2, no. 1, pp. 1–149.

Pope, Saxton T.
1918   Yahi archery. *University of California Publications in American Archaeology and Ethnology,* vol. 13, no. 3., pp. 103–52.
1923   A study of bows and arrows. *Ibid.,* vol. 13, no. 9, pp. 329–414.

Pradel, L.
1958   Du racloir au biface, formes intermédiaires. *Bulletin de la Société Préhistorique Française,* vol. 55, pp. 64–70.

Profe, O.
1914   Vorgeschichtliche Jagd. *Mannus, Zeitschr. für Vorge-schichte,* vol. 6, pp. 107–34.

Ramendo, L.
1963   Les galets aménagés de Reggan (Sahara). *Libyca,* vol. II, pp. 43–73.

Renfrew, C., J. C. Dixon, and J. R. Cann
1966   Obsidian and early cultural contact in the Near East. *Proceedings of the Prehistoric Society,* Cambridge, The University Press, vol. 32, pp. 30–72.

Robinson, T. Radcliffe
1938   A survival of flake-technique in Southern Rhodesia. *Man,* vol. 38, no. 224.

Robinson, J. T., and R. J. Mason
1957   Occurrence of stone artifacts with Australopithecus at Sterkfontein. *Nature,* vol. 180, no. 4585, pp. 521–24.

Sackett, James R.
1966   *Quantitative analysis of Upper Paleolithic stone tools.* In J. D. Clark & F. C. Howell (eds.), Recent studies in paleo-anthropology. *American Anthropologist,* vol. 68, no. 2, part 2, 394 pp.

Sanger, David
1968   The High River microblade industry, Alberta. *Plains An-
          thropologist,* 13–41, pp. 190–208.

Sankalia, H. D.
1963   *Prehistory and protohistory in India and Pakistan.* Bom-
          bay, V. G. Boght.
1964   *Stone age tools. Their techniques, names and probable
          functions.* Poona, Deccan College.
1967   The socioeconomic significance of the lithic blade industry
          of Navdatoli, Madhya Pradesh, India. *Current Anthro-
          pology,* vol. 8, no. 3, pp. 262–68.

Schleicher, C.
1927   Une industrie qui disparaît. La taille des silex modernes.
          L'Homme Préhistorique, vol. 14, pp. 113–33.

Sellers, George E.
1885   Observations on stone-chipping. *Annual Report of the
          Smithsonian Institution for 1885, pt. I,* pp. 871–91.

Semenov, Sergei A.
1964   *Prehistoric technology; an experimental study of the oldest
          tools and artifacts from traces of manufacture and wear.*
          London, Cory, Adams and Mackay, 211 pp.

Shippee, J. M.
1963   Was flint annealed before flaking? *Plains Anthropologist,*
          vol. 8, no. 22.

Shotton, F. W.
1963   Petrological examination. In *Science and Archaeology,* Don
          Brothwell and Eric Higgs, eds., pp. 482–88.

Singer, Charles, E. J. Holmyard, and A. R. Hall
1954   *A history of technology. Vol. I, From early times to fall
          of ancient empires.* New York and London, Oxford Uni-
          versity Press, 827 pp., 36 plates.

Skertchly, Sidney B. J.
1879   Manufacture of gun-flints; the method of excavation for
          flint, the age of palaeolithic man. London, *Memoirs of the
          geological survey,* England and Wales.

Skinner, H. D.
1948   Chisel, wedge, axe and adze. *Antiquity,* Gloucester, Eng-
          land, vol. 22, pp. 208–10.

Smith, G. V.
1893   The use of flint blades to work pine wood. *Annual Report
          for 1891. Smithsonian Institution,* pp. 601–5.

Smith, Philip E. L.
1964　　　The Solutrean Culture. *Scientific American,* vol. 211, no. 2, pp. 86–94.
1966a　　*Le Solutréen en France.* Publications de l'Institut de Préhistoire, mémoire no. 5, Université de Bordeaux, Bordeaux, imprimerie Delmas, 449 pp.
1966b　　Lithic technology; report on conference, November 25–28, 1964, Les Eyzies. *Current Anthropology,* vol. 7, no. 5, pp. 592–93.

Société Préhistorique Française
1954　　　Les grandes civilisations préhistoriques de la France. Livre jubilaire 1904–1954. *Bulletin de la Société Préhistorique Française,* vol. 51, fasc. 8, pp. 1–111.

Sollas, W. J.
1924　　　*Ancient hunters and their modern representatives,* 3rd ed. rev. New York, Macmillan, 689 pp.

Sonnenfeld, J.
1962　　　Interpreting the function of primitive implements. *American Antiquity,* vol. 28, no. 1, pp. 56–65.

Sonneville-Bordes, Denise de
1960　　　*Le paléolithique supérieur en Périgord.* 2 vols., Bordeaux, Imprimerie Delmas, 558 pp.
1961　　　*L'Age de la pierre.* Paris, Presses Universitaires de France, 128 pp.
1967　　　*La préhistoire moderne.* Périgueux, Pierre Fanlac, 128 pp., 47 figs., 140 photographs.

Sonneville-Bordes, D., and J. Perrot
1953　　　Essai d'adaptation des méthodes statistiques au Paléolithique. I. Grattoirs. II. Outils solutréens. *Bulletin de la ciété Préhistorique Française,* vol. 50, no. 5–6, pp. 323–333.
1954　　　Lexique typologique du Paléolithique supérieur. Outillage lithique. I. Grattoirs, II. Outils solutréens. *Bulletin de la Société Préhistorique Française,* vol. 51, no. 7, pp. 327–35.
1955　　　Lexique typologique du Paléolithique supérieur. Outillage lithique. III. Outils composites. Perçoirs. *Bulletin de la Société Préhistorique Française,* vol. 52, no. 1–2, pp. 76–79.
1956a　　Lexique typologique du Paléolithique supérieur. Outillage lithique. IV. Burins. *Bulletin de la Société Préhistorique Française,* vol. 53, no. 7–8, pp. 408–12.
1956b　　Lexique typologique du Paléolithique supérieur. Outillage lithique. V. Outillage à bord abattu. VI. Pièces tronquées.

VII. Lames retouchées. VIII. Pièces variées. IX. Outillage lamellaire. Pointe azilienne. *Bulletin de la Société Préhistorique Française,* vol. 53, no. 9, pp. 547–59.

Squier, Robert J.
1953   The manufacture of flint implements by the Indians of northern and central California. Papers on California Archaeology: 19–20, pp. 15–32. *Berkeley, The University of California Archaeological Survey.*

Strahm, Christian
1961–62 Geschäftete Dolchklingen des Spätneolithikums. *Jahrbuch des Bernischen Museums in Bern,* vols. 41 and 42, pp. 447–77.

Swanson, Earl H.
1966   An introduction to Crabtree's experiments in flint knapping. *Tebiwa, The Journal of the Idaho State University Museum,* vol. 9, no. 1, pp. 1–2.
1968   *The shadow of man.* Film showing D. E. Crabtree quarrying obsidian and duplicating stone tools found at aboriginal quarries in Oregon. Color & sound. Idaho State Museum, Pocatello. 28½ minutes long.

Taute, Wolfgang
1965   Retoucheure aus Knochen, Zahnebein und Stein von Mittel Paläolithikum bis zum Neolithikum. *Fundberichte aus Schwaben,* vol. 17, Stuttgart, pp. 76–102.

Tendron, G.
1949   La photographie monochromatique en préhistoire. *La Nature,* no. 3175, pp. 344–45.

Thomson, Donald F.
1964   Some wood and stone implements of the Bindibu tribe of central Western Australia. *Proceedings of the Prehistoric Society,* vol. 30, pp. 400–23.

Tixier, Jacques.
1963   *Typologie de l'épipaléolithique du Maghreb,* no. 2. Paris, Arts et Métiers Graphiques, 211 pp.

Ucko, Peter J., and Andrée Rosenfeld
1967   *Palaeolithic cave art.* London, Weidenfeld & Nicolson, 256 pp.

140 *Bibliography*

University of California
1967   *Early stone tools.* Film showing François Bordes flaking
           some lower and middle Paleolithic stone tools. Color and
           sound. Berkeley, Department of Anthropology, 20 min-
           utes long.

Valoch, Karel
1968   Evolution of the Paleolithic in Central and Eastern Europe.
           Current Anthropology, vol. 9, no. 5, pp. 351–90.

Vayson de Pradenne, A.
1932   *Les fraudes en archéologie préhistorique avec quelques
           exemples de comparaison en archéologie générale et sci-
           ences naturelles.* Paris, Emile Nourry, 676 pp.

Vértes, L.
1965   Typology of the Buda industry: a pebble tool industry
           from the Hungarian Lower Palaeolithic. *Quaternaria,* vol.
           7, pp. 185–195.

Walker, D., and Ann de G. Sieveking
1962   The Palaeolithic industry of Kota Tampan, Perak. *Pro-
           ceedings of the Prehistoric Society,* vol. 28, pp. 103–39.

Warren, S. H.
1914   The experimental investigation of flint fracture and its
           application to the problems of human implements. *Journal
           of the Royal Anthropological Institute,* vol. 44, pp. 412–50.

Waterbolk, H. T.
1968   Food production in prehistoric Europe. *Science,* vol. 162,
           pp. 1093–1102.

Watson, William.
1956   *Flint implements.* London, published by the Trustees of the
           British Mus., 81 pp.

White, Carmel
1967   Early Stone axes in Arnhem land. *Antiquity,* vol. 41, pp.
           149–52.

Willey, Gordon R.
1966   *An introduction to American archaeology. Volume I,
           North and Middle America.* Englewood Cliffs, New Jersey,
           Prentice-Hall. 526 pp.

Wilmsen, Edwin N.
1968a   Functional analysis of flaked stone artifacts. *American
           Antiquity,* vol. 33, no. 2, pp. 156–61.

1968b   Lithic analysis in paleoanthropology. *Science,* vol. 161, pp. 982–87.

Wormington, Hanna M.
1957   *Ancient Man in North America.* 4th ed. Denver Museum of Natural History, 322 pp.

Wilson, Thomas.
1899   Arrowpoints, spearheads and knives of prehistoric times. *Annual Report of the United States National Museum, Smithsonian Institution 1897,* pt. 1, pp. 811–988, 201 figs. 65 pls.

Zeuner, Frederick E.
1958   *Dating the past.* 3rd ed. rev. and enlarged. London, Methuen Co., Ltd., 516 pp., 27 pls.
1959   *The Pleistocene period; its climate, chronology and faunal successions.* London, Hutchison, 447 pp., pls., maps.
1964   *A history of domesticated animals.* London, Hutchison, 360 pp., ill.

Index

Prepared flake nuclei, 31, 38, 39, 56, 57, fig. 12
Pressure flaking, 12, 80, 93, 111, fig. 3–7, 8, figs. 35 to 39
Proto-biface, 20
Punch and hammer flaking, 55, 56, 80, 93, fig. 3–4, 6
Punjab, 20

Quartzite, 10, 17
Querns, 105

Raclette, fig. 22–9
Rectangle bladelets, fig. 22–36
Retouch, 16, 57, 65, 80, fig. 3–5, 7, 8, figs. 38, 39
Retouchoir, 80, fig. 3–7, figs. 38, 39
Rhyolite, 10
Ridged blade. *See* Crested blade
Ripples, 12, 19, 76, fig. 2
Riss glaciation, 19, fig. 1
Riss-Würm interglacial, 38

Sankalia, H. D., xii
Sawing, stone. *See* Stone sawing
Scrapers, 19, 43, 44, 68. *See* End-scrapers, Keeled scrapers, Nosed scrapers, Side scrapers
Sedentism. *See* Dwellings and settlements
Semenov, S. A., 42
Settlements. *See* Dwellings and settlements
Shouldered points, 76, fig. 22–8, 39, figs. 35, 36, 37
Siberia, 93
Side scrapers, 39, 45, fig. 18
Silcrete, 10
Siliceous stone tool materials, 9–12
Silicified stone tool materials, 10
Sinew, 7
Skin, 7, 95
Skis, 95
Slash and burn or swidden cultivation, 95, 96
Sledges, 95
Soft hammer percussion, 25, 27, 55, 76, figs. 8, 11
Solutrean, 76, 80, 86
Southwest Asia, 87, 89, 92, 93, 95, 105
Spain, 76, 108
Spears, wooden, 7, 21, 42, 44, 47
Spear throwers, 72, 86, 92
Specialized tools, use of, 46
Spiennes, 104
Stone Age, 2, 3, 5
Stone pecking, 47, 104–6, 111, fig. 51
Spear points, bone, 6, 47, 65, 72, 86, 92, fig. 41
Spear points, stone, 21, 39, 43–45, 65, 72, 76, 80, fig. 22–2, 4, 5, 7, 8, 11, 31, 39
Stone battering. *See* Stone pecking
Stone flaking. *See* Direct and indirect percussion flaking, Pressure flaking

Stone grinding, 5, 93, 96, 99, 101, 102, 104–6, 108, 111, figs. 43 to 50, 52, 53
Stone quarries, 106
Stone sawing, 42, 106, 108
Stone tool materials, hardness of, 9, 10; homogeneity of, 11, 12; tenacity of, 10, 11
Stone tools, determining uses of, xi, 39, 41–47
Stone tools, evolution of, 6, 56, 57, 86, 93, 95
Stone tools, experimentation with, xi, 41, 42
Stone tools, importance of, 6, 7, 8, 111
Strangulated blade, fig. 22–3
Strike-a-light, 111
Striking platform, 19, 24, 27, 51, 55, 76, figs. 2, 7, 11, 14, 53
Support, types of, 13, fig. 3
Swidden cultivation. *See* Slash and burn or Swidden cultivation

Tata, 49
Tanged stone points, 65, fig. 22–5, 11, 31, fig. 31
Tell Ubeidiya, 19
Three Age system, 3
Threshing sledges, frontispiece, 108
Thunderstones. *See* Ceraunias
Timber work, 93, 96, 99
Torralba, 7
Tool needs, basic, 42
Tranchet technique, 95
Triangle bladelets, fig. 22–35
Truncated blades, 57, 68, 69, 71, 72, fig. 22–20, 21, 22
Turkey, frontispiece, 108
Turning-the-edge, 24, 76, fig. 7
Teyjat points, fig. 22–11

Unifacial points, fig. 22–7
Uses of stone tools, determination. *See* Stone tools, determining uses of

Vallonet, 19
Vértesszöllös, 19
Volcanic stone tool materials, 10, 80
Volgu, xii, 76

Waste. *See* Débitage
Ways of life, 5, 6; Lower Paleolithic, 17, 37, 38; Middle Paleolithic, 48–50; Upper Paleolithic, 50, 86–88; Mesolithic, 88, 89, 92, 106; Neolithic, 95, 96, 106–8
Wear, study of traces of, xi, 17, 42, 45
Weaving, 95
Wedges, 17, 71, 96
Wild plant gathering, 92. *See* Hunting, fishing and gathering
Willow leaves, Solutrean, 76
Wooden implements. *See* Bone, antler and wooden implements
Würm glaciation, 48, fig. 1